To my wife Patti and our four children who shared in our journey of faith. I am proud of their life choices.

Published by MT Press
© 2019 by Casey Sabella
Published 2018
Third edition

ISBN: 9781791613013

Cover design by Hih7, hih7.com
Edited by Caitlin Vaichus
Printed in the United States

For More Information:

MTP Books
100 Sage Drive
Waterbury, CT 06704

SPIRITUAL

ABUSE

*How to Identify and Break Free from Toxic
Churches Without Losing Your Faith*

By Casey M. Sabella

FREE COURSE GUIDE

To help guide you through the issues raised in this book, I created a free course you can access online. This includes worksheets and bonus audio content to help you sort out your circumstance.

At the end of each chapter, I will remind you to download the next module to help you sort through the issues raised. Download each module @ ministerstoolbox.com/free-courses.

If this book and course help you, consider leaving me an honest review @ Amazon.com. It only takes a few seconds and can support hundreds of other people recovering from toxic church experiences.

Listen to Spiritual Abuse: How To Identify And Break Free From Toxic Churches Without Losing Your Faith on Audiobooks.com or download this edition onto your Kindle device.

TABLE OF CONTENTS

INTRODUCTION

Churches are supposed to be safe places you can visit to hear the Good News about Jesus. They are supposed to be places where you make friends and work together to impact your community and the world.

When I became a Christian in my late teens, the whole world changed in a matter of seconds. I went from agnostic to believer and started a journey that has lasted over forty years.

The church I first attended became my family in many ways. I loved the teaching, music, atmosphere, and community of fellow believers. In those early days, we saw God move in miraculous ways as the church grew each year.

Unfortunately, things changed over time. My church stopped being a place I loved to attend and eventually became a place I hoped no one would attend! The teaching became complicated and confusing. We still believed the Bible, but we also accepted principles that did not square with scripture.

The pastor changed too. He began to take actions that seemed more designed to enhance his image than advance the mission of the church. Some of you can relate to this because you struggle with similar issues yourself.

The book you are reading is the third iteration of a book I published in 1992 with much-needed updates. It first appeared under the title, *When A Church Goes Bad*, five years after leaving the church I loved. Initially, the book created an overwhelming response throughout the country.

During more than thirty-five radio and television interviews, I spoke to many who were certain I once attended *their* churches! They insisted I described events in their congregations to the letter and were stunned to learn they were mistaken.

I realized that the problems I described resemble practices in far too many churches. My goal then as now was to help people who face similar experiences find spiritual health.

What you are about to read is a true story. The names and some of the exact details surrounding the circumstances have been changed while preserving the narrative as accurately as possible.

My objective is not to expose anyone to ridicule or pain, but to provide a roadmap to individuals struggling with many of the same issues within their churches.

My prayer then as now is to help you regain your passion for God. Whatver negative experiences you have endured, He still restores broken people and re-forms them for His glory when we say, "yes."

-Casey

[Before you continue, download the Introduction course from ministerstoolbox.com/free-courses.]

MY JOURNEY OF FAITH

"...I was born at a very early age." Groucho Marx

The third son of five boys and one girl, I grew up in a good home. My mother was Irish Catholic. My father was a mix of Italian, Irish, and German. Discussions around the dinner table tended to be lively!

My dad clawed his way up from poverty to achieve executive status in a national company. We lived in a large suburban home, and my parents' dream of wealth gradually came true.

I will never forget the day dad came home with a shiny new Buick Electra 225. The car had a phone and electric windows. That was beyond cool to a kid in the 1960's. I mean, a real phone in a car? Wow.

The neighborhood kids and I spent hours playing with the new electric windows. It is wonder the battery did not wear out.

My two older brothers had red hair; no doubt the Irish genes came through. I was the first in our family to be born with black hair. This feature made me the odd man out when my younger brother also turned up with red on top.

Speaking of that younger brother, he was a major problem for me.

Mom gave birth about every two years. When she was about to deliver her fourth son, my parents thought it would be a good idea to ship me off to my father's parents to take care of me for a few days.

In retrospect, this did not turn out to be their wisest decision.

At just two yrs., I did not know my paternal grandparents very well. My father dropped me off at their home in another state. In an unfamiliar house far away from home, I could not comprehend why I'd been abandoned and given to strangers.

What had I done wrong?

I cried a lot. My grandpa's solution was to take me places to show off one of his grandsons. He drove me to Brooklyn to introduce me to his buddies at the barbershop.

They were delighted to see me. I cannot say the feeling was mutual. Old men pinched my cheeks, communicating in those funny voices adults typically make to toddlers.

I say this like I remembered it because I do. At barely two years old, the images remain lucid even though I was young.

My hair was a little too long and curly to suit my grandpa's taste. He decided to make me look more like a boy by granting me my first haircut. Strapped to a barber chair, a strange man used electric cutters to change my appearance.

Good times.

Finally, my little brother was born, and I returned home. My grandparents and I came into our large kitchen. The new baby lay in his bassinet. Everyone crowded around him, anxious to see the new arrival. Even at two years old, this new reality did not escape my attention.

Finally, my mom bent down to welcome me into her arms. I did not move. She motioned for me to come, but I did not budge. As she drew near to hug me, I put both hands up to her face and pushed her away.

I share this heartwarming little story not to cast aspersions on my brother or parents. I do so because this event became a significant moment in my development.

Somewhere deep in my consciousness, I made up my mind to survive, even if that meant going it alone. This perception governed how I viewed the world from then on.

Something else also occurred. I decided my younger brother was public enemy number one. From this moment, I disconnected from both of my parents on a certain level. The enemy of my soul planned this event to shape and twist my future for his purposes.

From an early age, I remember hating my parents. Almost daily, I would get stomach aches from the tension inside. My view screen of the world made me a difficult kid to raise. If the way was white, then I went black; if the plan was order, I went for chaos.

By contrast, my younger brother was calm and easy to get along with. That fact only added to my contempt for him. Though he tried to hang around with me as any younger brother would, I hated being "stuck" with him.

Over time, my younger brother developed a severe stuttering problem. I have little doubt I was the direct cause. He never finished a sentence without my cutting him off in some way.

While attending public school, my temperament did not make me amenable to making lots of friends. I possessed almost no social skills, which is understandable, given my worldview. As a result, I tended to be a loner.

Revenge of the Sixties

During this time, the culture of our society was in turmoil and about to explode. I will never forget that November day in third grade. Our teacher, Mrs. English reported through fresh tears that President Kennedy had died from an assassin's bullet. The world we knew was about to go through a cataclysmic transformation.

In a few years, the Beatles era gained momentum, and the Vietnam War started to ramp up. Thousands of young men left for war but came home in coffins draped with the American flag. The new President, LBJ faced turbulent times ahead.

Young people questioned social mores. Marijuana and LSD became the new ways to check out of the "establishment." Rebellion against authority - especially the police - became commonplace.

A month before my thirteenth birthday, the culture rocked with the announcement that Martin Luther King had been gunned down. Two months later, candidate Robert Kennedy, brother to former President Kennedy experienced the same fate. Civil unrest and violence in the streets erupted on every television screen.

Most cities needed extra police to manage protests against the war. United States culture was in upheaval, and no one knew what would happen next.

The music mirrored the culture and called for radical change. The Rolling Stones were young. Jim Morrison, Janis Joplin, and Jimi Hendrix introduced the world to unique, psychedelic music styles encouraging drug experimentation. Young people turned on to drugs, choosing lifestyles that rejected societal norms.

My eldest brother, a talented musician in his own right, was swept up into this dawn of the Woodstock generation. *"Free love," "Give peace a chance"* and *"Who's to say what's normal?"* became the most oft-repeated phrases from the lips of college students.

Communes sprung up on the West Coast of the U.S. as "hippies" lived and farmed together. They grew their own food to get back to a more "natural" lifestyle while practicing various eastern philosophies.

In the midst of all of this chaos and upheaval, something unique also happened: the birth of the Jesus Movement.

It arrived quite unexpectedly, and churches were thoroughly unprepared to meet the challenges it created. Sovereignly overnight, thousands of dropouts, hippies, and radicals heard the gospel, dropped their anger against society and obeyed the call to follow Jesus.

Trying To Find My Way Home

By age fifteen, I was already devoted to the study and practice of eastern mysticism. While studying under a yoga instructor, I embraced the occult and Kung-Fu Karate.

At home, things could not have been much worse.

Due to many explosive arguments with my parents, I left home at 16 years old to live at the Karate dojo. My goal was to devote myself to Kung-Fu and eastern philosophies entirely.

This move only lasted a few weeks because I ran out of money! However, my pursuit of this lifestyle intensified.

As my seventeenth birthday approached, I was a hot mess. Conflicted by anger, blinders started to fall from my eyes. At the dojo, I saw broken relationships, selfishness and even rage on display from each of my mentors. I joined to gain inner peace and answers to my question, but my instructors did not practice what they preached.

My vegan yogi abandoned his life of celibacy and self-control to eat hamburgers and sleep with several of his students. My King-Fu master's top students got arrested for violence - one for manslaughter! This did not match the disciplined life of serenity I was supposed to receive.

I had come to believe that eastern philosophies led to tranquility and world peace. Instead, I saw that my teachers exhibited flawed human behaviors like everyone else.

On a personal level, two dating relationships ended in ugly breakups, primarily due to my self-centeredness. In addition, my friends could be counted on half of my right hand.

I continued to carry an enormous amount of hatred for my parents and many others for various reasons. Trained in Kung-Fu, I became a fighter looking for a fight, verbally or otherwise.

My father and I argued constantly. I despised him and looked for any opportunity to be absent from the house.

One day, my parents received a phone call from my eldest brother, in college out in Portland, Oregon. He called to inform our family that he left his former lifestyle to become a Christian.

Huh?

My parents did not know how to respond. As Catholics, we were already Christian from our religious perspective. What did he mean?

He went on to explain that he had given his life to Jesus Christ. Explaining that he repented of his sins, my brother asked my parents to forgive him.

I think my parents were embarrassed, not knowing what to think. Finally, they concluded that their first-born son *needed* this change. The music culture to which he belonged gave his life no structure or purpose. Christianity perhaps would change that. For my part, I thought he'd gone off the deep end.

Meanwhile, turmoil accelerated in my personal life. Nothing meant anything to me anymore. My workouts at the dojo slowed to a halt.

As summer approached, I thought I would find a job and earn lots of cash.

Around that time, this same brother called to invite me to join him on the West Coast for a month. The invitation seemed odd. Why would I want to do that?

My father, overhearing the conversation asked me who I was speaking with. When I told him about my brother's invitation, he immediately offered to pay for the flight.

Having no other commitments, I said "yes," and wondered what I was getting myself into.

Shortly after that, I landed in South Portland, OR and met some of the "Jesus People." My brother called them his "brothers and sisters." Very weird. As I arrived, they were playing music in the park. I sat in the crowd, realizing I had no place to go!

Since my brother was the only person I knew, I followed him wherever he went. That night, we set off to attend a local Pentecostal church where approximately five hundred young people gathered to worship. Things got *weird* for me when I saw the vast majority lifting their hands in praise to God. Stranger still was that they seemed to be enjoying it!

My religious upbringing was more like a mausoleum than a circus, so all this baffled me. My idea of a church service involved a quiet cave-like atmosphere where no one spoke unless repeating prayers at the behest of the minister.

This Pentecostal church was multi-ethnic, multi-generational and dynamic. People sang and clapped to live music as if they truly enjoyed themselves. Several raised their hands with eyes closed, lost in prayer. Truthfully, it freaked me out.

Afterward, we stopped at Denny's restaurant to eat. I asked my brother and his friends lots of questions. Their answers all seemed to focus on knowing Christ personally which seemed foreign to me. In the end, I told them they could believe whatever they wanted, but that their beliefs weren't for me.

The Jesus I Never Knew

While in Oregon, I stayed with my brother in a large two family house. Several men shared expenses and accommodations. Some were students at the university; others held jobs, and some would sleep there for one night before moving on.

The men prayed together, beginning each day with devotions from the King James Bible. A church elder took responsibility for the management of the house. This gave me a front row seat to watch how Christian men lived.

On my second day, we went to a church member's home that needed construction work. We all pitched in to help pour concrete for a walkway. It was hard work. Our pay was a great lunch and the thankfulness of our host.

When we arrived back at the apartment, dinner was waiting for us. A few of the women from the church volunteered to make a meal for us. The humility and kindness of that act affected me. I took note that they did not wait around for compliments - just served and left.

The man whose home we repaired led us in grace before the meal. I was familiar with *grace*. As a Catholic family, the nightly blessing before a meal was easy. *"Bless us, O Lord, and these your gifts, which we are about to receive from your bounty. Through Christ our Lord, Amen."* We could recite this sentence at the speed of light without understanding a single word!

He did not pray that way. Instead, he acted like he was talking to God. I opened my eyes to see if anyone else was in the room! His words were heartfelt, reasonable, and without religious wording.

A few days later, my brother's church hosted a potluck dinner. I had no interest in attending, so I asked about *my* meal. My brother informed me that "dinner" was available only at church.

Could I attend the potluck, but *not* go to service? No problem.

After dinner, several church members invited me to the service. I did not want to go. I also had no other plans, so why not?

The music was contemporary, which was good. I don't think I could have tolerated old hymns. After the announcements, the preacher stood up to speak. He spoke intensely as he quoted one scripture after another.

I do not recall a word he said. Not a lick of it made sense to me, as he quoted various scripture verses. Since it was a Pentecostal-type church, he tended to move around a lot while he preached. All I could think about was getting home to bed!

When he finished, he gave what I learned was an "altar call," inviting people up front to give their lives to Jesus. Within this framework, he uttered these words: *"If there is a mountain in your life and you're a Christian, God can move it."*

To this day I cannot explain why those words affected me that night. I could not perceive a mountain in my mind, yet I knew it was there. When he said those words, I thought to myself, *"Well, this does not apply to me, because I am not a Christian."*

At that moment, he spoke again. *"Even if you're not a Christian here tonight, and there is a mountain in your life, God can move it."* Suddenly, I felt like God shined his spotlight on me!

The preacher called people to the front for prayer. No one moved. Internally, conflict raged. I sensed something powerful happening to me, but there was no chance that *I* would go forward!

He finally gave up pleading with the congregation, and we closed in song. In Pentecostal churches at that time, members raised their hands while singing in worship. I joined them by raising my hand for just a brief moment.

I prayed to God: *"If you're real, and you can show me, I will follow you."* At that moment, something changed.

The hate that dominated my life vanished. I mean it was gone! Furthermore, I knew that Jesus was God, but could not tell you how. This was unique.

My brother spotted me raising a hand and came around me with other members, excited that I had become a Christian. I was even more bewildered. Had I? Had I become a follower of Christ? Was it that simple?

I went back to the men's house scratching my head. This was great and all, but I wanted more evidence that God was real.

Over the next few days, I prayed. I asked God for wisdom, understanding, and answers to various questions. It would take much too long to recount, but prayers started getting answered in extraordinary ways.

The only bibles in the house were in the King James version, translated in the 1600s. Strangely enough, though an average student and poor reader, I did not struggle to understand it. *Thees, thous,* and *thithers* helped me remember scripture better.

Like someone lost in a desert, I couldn't drink in enough scripture to be satisfied. The sheer practicality of Christ's teaching astounded me. I felt like someone turned my brain to "on" after being "off" my whole life.

Returning home a month later, my father looked confounded. His third son forsook Karate and eastern mysticism to confess Christ as his Lord and Savior.

My brother's conversion made sense to his way of thinking. Dad equated drug use and the music scene as disorder and chaos. His eldest son's conversion offered structure and moral clarity.

When I sat in front of him for the first time as a believer, he was dumbfounded. How did his argumentative, hateful third son transform into a Christian? Since it did not fit his prescribed ideas about religion, he was unsure what to think.

Once I got resettled, my brother set about finding a place for me to go church before he returned to Oregon. After several possibilities, he found a Christian coffee house forty-five minutes from my home.

This new place, Good News Chapel would become my new spiritual family.

[Before you continue, please download chapter one from ministerstoolbox.com/free-courses.]

GOOD NEWS CHAPEL

"Give me a J!" the pastor shouted.

"J!"

"Give me an E!"

"E!" the crowd shouted back.

"Give me an S!"

"S!"

"Give me a U!"

"U!"

"Give me another S!"

"S!"

"What's that spell?" the pastor yelled.

"JESUS!!!" came the thunderous response.

"Louder!!!!!"

"JESUS!!!!!!!!"

This began a typical Friday night at Good News Chapel. A hundred young people crammed into the small, storefront coffeehouse shouted the "Jesus Cheer" with enthusiasm matching a Super Bowl crowd.

The faces in the crowd were young, mostly between 15-25 years old. Some sat around tables. (They were large wooden spools the phone company discarded that once wrapped large cable lines.) Others sat shoulder to shoulder on the thinly carpeted floor for this weekly night of celebration lasting two to four hours.

Oriental paper shades dimmed the glare from the bare light bulbs dangling from the ceiling. The year was 1972.

Young people met to hang out in places where psychedelic posters plastered the walls and rock and roll bands played into the early morning. It did not matter if the place looked good on the outside, so long as the inside was alive with activity.

Good News Chapel was slightly different. The posters told of the need to find God and the music's central message: experience a personal relationship with Jesus Christ.

Between songs, some raised their hands in the hope of being asked to share what Christ had done for them that week. Teens wept as they shared what it was like to live a life blurred by alcohol and drug addiction. Others shared about the emptiness they experienced from promiscuous sex.

The goal of each meeting was to present Jesus as the only One to bring real peace to people who welcomed Him. The joy and excitement on each face infected anyone who attended. At times, parents would even come to declare the positive changes they saw in their children.

Around 10 p.m., everyone would smell the aroma of coffee wafting in from the next room. Closing the meeting in prayer, the "Jesus people" filed out of the main room, grabbed a coffee and a free doughnut to continue sharing with the many guests who assembled each night.

Sometimes the conversations lasted until midnight. Often these guests would be seen bowing their heads to receive Christ as their savior when one of the "regulars" led them in prayer.

Good News Chapel became the envy of many of the more established churches in the region. We were effective in reaching people no one else wanted: runaways, drug users, alcoholics, and the homeless. Through Good News, young people found their way to God.

Over the next several years, Good News Chapel tripled in size. Outreach centers opened in several cities throughout the state. Hundreds of young people met Christ through a gospel preached in the street language of the day to become "new creatures in Christ."[1]

We opened up live-in centers for men and women and hosted seminars in hotels attended by large crowds each month. In time, we rented large civic center venues to feature national Christian speakers. Good News Chapel was becoming our state's first megachurch.

Today, all remnants of this once-great ministry are gone. The chapel is now a wood-working shop where a housing contractor conducts his business. The ministry lives only in the memory of those who once attended.

Good News Chapel was my church. A newborn in Christ when I first walked through the door, it became the central focus of my time and energy for over fifteen years. Good News was where I:

- Learned basic Christian doctrine.
- Trained towards leadership.

---

[1] II Corinthians 5:17

- Became ordained as a pastor.
- Met my wife.
- Dedicated my firstborn daughter.

I entered Good News Chapel as a seventeen-year-old teenager. I left as the thirty-two-year-old father of a growing family. Good News was my life!

This powerful and dynamic church deteriorated over time. These first chapters tell the story of how that happened and why.

Before we begin, what about you? Do you belong to a *problem church* or merely a *church with problems*? The difference is significant.

Every church has problems and challenges. Those featured in the New Testament were no different. The apostles wrote letters to address these problems. Since we live in a fallen world populated by flawed humans, challenges in every church are universal.

Today, many Christians leave churches because:

- The church is too small.
- The church is too large.
- The preacher is not exciting enough.
- The church lacks enough programs for children or youth.

- There is no coffee hour.
- They don't like the music, wallpaper...etc.

If these are your struggles, I probably can't help you. Someone led you to believe that the nature of true Christianity is comfort. It is not, and the church can be messy at times. All churches have problems, and we should not be willing to break relationships over trivial issues.

By contrast, I want to help Christ-followers who genuinely love God and their church, but have become deeply conflicted. Recent decisions or practices by their leaders cause them to question whether the church is still legitimate.

Problem churches, like the one I will describe, have gotten so off track they are no longer in sync with Christ's mission. They cannot be restored without a complete overhaul.

Do not use this book as a weapon to criticize your church, but as a guide to make godly decisions. I aim to help Christians address issues that can be fixed, or break free of systems that have become abusive and now run contrary to scripture.

I wish my story were an isolated one. Many churches continue to fall into error by losing their focus on the true Head of the Church.

There are a variety of churches and denominations throughout the world in decline because they have lost sight of the centrality of Christ. Some drift further to violate the same biblical principles we once did.

Some of you may have left your church, disillusioned by the hypocrisy and human frailty you witnessed. Now, you waste time and emotional energy reliving bitter memories of past hurts. You left, but never quite recovered.

I get it.

We're going to talk about things most don't want to address. We will look at scripture to discern what constitutes a church over which Christ is Lord. We will ask some essential questions designed to help you forgive those who hurt you. We will also examine biblical solutions to help you back to spiritual health.

One final thing to consider. The events you are about read about occurred decades ago. The teenager who joined Good News at seventeen is today a grandfather with the perspective of time. As you read about Good News Chapel, keep in mind it's historical setting. These were the days:

- Before anyone ever heard of Bill Gates, Steve Jobs or the Internet.
- When Christian television was in its infancy.
- Before the *PTL Club* scandal.

- When *Jimmy Swaggart* was #1 evangelist in the country.
- You could fill your car with gas for just a few dollars.
- No one ever bought coffee except to brew it at home.
- When "made in Japan" meant low quality.
- When oversight of churches by the government was almost nonexistent.

Understanding the time in our history will give you a better context for what you are about to read. Please know that I currently serve as a pastor. I love the Church of Jesus Christ and have given my entire life to promoting the gospel in every way possible.

Christ is everything to me. While I sympathize with those who have been hurt or abused by their leaders, I don't support those who love to criticize every weakness they see in churches. Leaders need our prayers, financial support, and love. We all have faults and weaknesses, so I am not writing this book to undermine the Church that Christ loves.

Leadership is both a calling and a solemn responsibility. God appoints leaders to advance His purposes on earth. No one is above accountability for their actions.

Now, let me introduce you to my former pastor.

[Before you continue, please download chapter two from ministerstoolbox.com/free-courses.]

PASTOR MIKE

I f you needed proof that God could change a life, you did not have to look further than the pulpit at Good News Chapel. Pastor Mike was a towering figure of a man. Standing over six feet tall at two hundred sixty pounds, he was an imposing figure with a deep and powerful voice.

Mike grew up in the 1950s watching Elvis Presley's meteoric rise to success. Every teenage boy back then learned how to play the guitar like Elvis, hoping to achieve similar results. Mike joined a band, playing nightclubs and bars while looking for the "big break." It never came.

Footloose and single, Mike lived life in the fast lane with an insatiable appetite for wine, women, and song. Every night was a party. Every morning was a hangover.

Then he met Christine.

Christine was the sort of girl who made Mike believe he could settle down and become a respectable family man. They married, and he gave it his best effort.

He secured a job selling used cars as they started to build a life together. Soon, a baby was on the way and then another. Because of Mike's take-charge nature, he got raises at work and set his sights on financial success.

Before long, a promotion to general manager increased their standard of living. The money flowed in, but their marriage changed. It wasn't long before Christine realized her new husband was up to his old tricks, even with their third child on the way.

Women showed up at the dealership but had more than buying a car on their minds. Even his new role as a dad did not keep him from a roving eye. Late nights at the office became opportunities to break his marriage vows and blame it on an increased workload.

Christine was on to him. Dishes and small appliances came sailing through the air designed to let Mike know his wife was no fool. Screaming arguments signaled to the neighbors that their marriage was falling apart.

Devastated, Christine considered divorce. She felt torn up inside about the prospect of raising their kids without a father.

One day, Christine heard a local pastor preaching on the radio. She called the phone number he gave, and soon the pastor and his wife came to her home for a visit.

Having nowhere to turn, Christine invited Jesus Christ into her heart and life. Everything changed. Instead of fighting, Christine started praying.

Mike came home to cooked meals and a woman who kept the dishes in the cabinet! He was stunned. What had happened to his wife?

About a month later, Mike couldn't sleep. He got up and lumbered downstairs to the kitchen. On the table sat a Bible. He opened it for the first time in his life and the verse he read pierced his heart. There at the table, with no one else around, Mike gave his heart to Christ.

Like Christine, Mike's life changed overnight. So did his career. Instead of lying to potential customers, he began telling them the truth about some of the cars on the lot. When he attempted to steer clients towards better cars, they did not trust him! Talk about irony!

Mike's sales plummeted. His co-workers wondered what had happened to him, mocking him behind his back.

Meanwhile, the pastor at his new church encouraged him to use his musical skills to form a gospel group and perform at worship services. This make-shift quartet of men gained local fame and notoriety for their inspiring ministry as they sang favorite hymns for small audiences.

Destiny Calls

One day Mike received a call from a Baptist preacher's wife. Heartened by Mike's zeal for God and his ability to relate to young people, she called to share a dream. Every night for a week, the woman dreamt about a famous local discotheque. The dream troubled her so much she wondered if God might be telling her something.

She asked Mike to investigate whether God wanted to reach this forgotten culture in their city.

Being the adventurous type, Mike arrived at *The Hole in the Wall* around midday. Inside, he found several teens using the dilapidated building as their partying hangout.

Mike shared Christ with them as they all gathered around. Then he told them that Jesus wanted to use their building. To his surprise, they agreed!

Mike arranged to use the discotheque on a night when nothing was scheduled. He challenged these tough street kids to invite their friends for a special event. Mike drove home wondering what God would do next.

Teenagers arrived from everywhere to hear how a former rock and roller came to know Jesus Christ. He invited kids to come to the front for prayer, and many responded asking Jesus to change their lives.

Weeks later, the owners of the building gave it to Mike outright. For two years, he used it as a Christian coffeehouse reaching many young people. Finally, the local building inspector condemned the building and ordered it torn down.

When I arrived at Good News Chapel, they were meeting in a new location about a mile or so from the original site. I jumped in with both feet.

As a growing community, we were enthusiastic to do whatever we felt God would have us do. Handing out literature in parks, restaurants, and street corners occupied most of our time.

Mike became my mentor. He wasn't the greatest preacher or teacher, but he possessed an incredible vision. He believed God could do anything. In those days, the Holy Spirit showed up in dramatic and often miraculous ways.

The mentoring I received at Mike's hand was serendipitous. I learned about ministry while we drove in the car or picked up supplies at the hardware store. These give-and-take chats between us imparted teaching that has shaped my thinking to this day.

The majority of churches in the region did not accept Good New Chapel's legitimacy. That never bothered us. We were a little proud of this rejection, wearing it as an invisible badge of honor.

Other churches seldom welcomed runaways or the homeless before 1972. We did. This superior attitude gave us the "right" to judge other churches and isolated us further.

Mike moved the coffeehouse toward a more typical church structure. He added Sunday services and selected elders and deacons from among the congregation.

Many teens grew into productive men and women. Boys cut off their long hair, and girls began to dress more modestly. Young people who had been living for their next fix, got off drugs, got jobs, and many times got married.

Over time our public image became more respectable in the community. "Grown-ups" began to take us more seriously and we liked the attention.

After attending the church for six months, Mike named me a deacon along with six others. I considered it a great honor. I organized my calendar around all church activities to become the finest deacon possible.

Changes Ahead

By the close of my senior year in high school, I was at a crossroads. All my life, my father emphasized the need to get a college education. He put money away for just that purpose.

Also, he fully expected me to follow him into the family business. I had no such desire. All I wanted to do was serve Jesus Christ. Therefore, I only applied to colleges within driving distance to Good News Chapel so I could attend services on the weekends.

July 1973 became the turning point in my life that forever altered my future. Mike received an invitation to speak two hundred miles north of us at a small rural church. He invited our worship team along, and since I played guitar, I was part of that team.

On the first night of our stay, Mike had an unusual dream. In his dream, people he had never seen appeared at the foot of his bed, each in need of physical healing. Mike reached out to pray for them, and they disappeared. When he awoke, Mike felt this dream confirmed that these meetings would be historic.

For two nights, Mike preached his heart out to small crowds. Nothing in his arsenal of sermons seemed to have any impact whatsoever. He felt discouraged and confused.

On the third night, each of the people in his dream showed up in the church building. Mike felt excited! He rose to preach and - nothing. His sermon fell flat again!

Frustrated, he cut his message short and invited everyone in the church up to the altar for prayer. The host pastor joined him and united with Mike they prayed over each person. The Holy Spirit showed up dramatically.

When this host pastor prayed for me, he said astounding things. He told me that at that moment, God was giving him a vision of my future. In the vision, he saw a light over my brain which he said was the Word of God. He told me that God would empower me to know and to teach the scriptures.

Moments later, as I sat near the altar, God spoke directly and plainly to me. I heard no audible voice, but the message became part of my immediate understanding as if I did. God communicated to me that He was calling me into ministry.

Mind you; I was eighteen years old.

As the meeting drew to a close, Mike stopped his benediction, jumped off the altar and came directly over to me. He said to the congregation, "There is just more thing we need to do." Joined by the other leaders, Mike said he believed God was calling me to full-time church ministry.

My response? *"I know."*

Upon returning home, my father and mother were not as exuberant as I. Though my father had permitted me to pursue my future as I wished, he advised me to go to college first. I declined, feeling it had nothing to do with church work. In the end, he consented to allow me to try this direction for six months.

From the moment God spoke that fateful day, something changed inside me. The Holy Spirit began to pour understanding into me far beyond my years or education.

Suddenly, I possessed a gift to teach the scriptures as if I had been doing so all my life. From that day forward, I remained keenly aware that this gift is not an acquired skill.

At the ripe old age of eighteen, I began serving Good News Chapel as an elder. What I lacked in training or experience, I made up in passion and dedication.

With this new responsibility, came a voracious hunger for reading and studying theology. I "studied to show myself approved." Mike gave me regular opportunities to address our growing church. Initially, no one expressed joy in that decision. Then, God would show up by His grace.

Whenever I taught, people grew in their faith. Begrudgingly at first, people with more years under their belts acknowledged the gift of teaching that transcended my lack of experience.

Good News Chapel multiplied due in large part to Mike's all-consuming vision. His strategy was to open coffeehouse-type centers throughout the state. My task was to investigate and research each new location.

Once secured, I helped renovate the rented space as needed. Then I put up posters all over town inviting residents to participate in a special night of music. Sometimes we handed out free tickets or paid for a local radio spot to hype the event.

On opening night, we would bring our band in to play live, and share testimonials of how Christ changed our lives. In time, a congregation would form.

Before long, a handful of young people would join in as I preached and taught the Bible. During that time, I learned a lot about the grace of God as He anointed many of the teachings shared from His Word.

Eventually, someone else in leadership from that locality would assume the leadership role. I would start all over in another city.

Around that time, Mike also conceived of the idea of printing a regional newspaper. Back in those days, you could purchase mailing lists from Christian magazines to establish a following.

We designed our first newspaper with testimonials about people from Good News and brought the finished product to a local newspaper to do a special printing for us. Ten thousand homes received our first edition, which advertised our services and shared Christ-centered teaching.

In concert with our growth and the popularity created by the newspaper, we rented hotel ballrooms to host multi-church meetings. By inviting national authors in to speak, many Christians from around the state came to hear about Good News and all we did with young people.

Ironically, though these events targeted the larger body of Christ, Mike had no meaningful relationship with other local pastors. The thought of uniting with other local leaders never crossed his mind.

Since the hotel meetings were enormously successful, Mike set his eyes on the largest civic center auditorium in the region. For two years, we hosted four days of meetings there. National leaders preached and taught from morning until night as thousands registered for these events.

My role on the team was to lead worship. At twenty-one years of age, I was playing in a Christian band to thousands of people. Truthfully, I felt like a rock star!

From every vantage point, we were poised to become our state's first mega-church.

[Before you continue, please download chapter three from ministerstoolbox.com/free-courses.]

THE SEEDS OF DESTRUCTION

In the mid-seventies, a new movement reached national prominence, later referred to as the *Shepherding Movement*. Five nationally-recognized church leaders came together to address a local moral failure. In time, this alliance continued conducting teaching seminars on a host of different controversial topics in the Christian community.

Eventually, they created a bi-monthly magazine entitled, *New Wine* that found its way to 140 countries. In a short while, they spearheaded a movement that influenced the world.

The goal of this movement was to bring needed teaching and focus to the Christian community. Every two months, we devoured New Wine's articles and ideas but never formally joined the movement. I was always excited when New Wine arrived in my mailbox and read it cover to cover.

Articles addressed practical Christian living: relationships in the family, financial responsibility and accountability, integrity in the workplace, and spiritual authority.

Over time, the emphasis on spiritual authority became the dominant feature of the magazine and the movement. Submission to human authority is a biblical principle.[2] In truth, you can never *become* a spiritual leader unless you learn to *serve* one.

However, understanding and applying submission to authority developed into an unbalanced theology. People became overly dependent on winning the approval of their pastor at all costs to demonstrate their willingness to submit.

As church leaders across the country applied this teaching, abuses by insecure leaders happened everywhere. Gradually, churches connected to the shepherding movement created members incapable of making even the smallest decisions without pastoral guidance.

I do not believe the founding leaders of the movement conspired towards this end. Most of the teaching in New Wine was honorable, but human natures gravitated toward authority as a means of wielding power.

At Good News, we taught wives to submit to their husbands without question. The same applied to employees

---

[2] Ephesians 5:21-30; Romans 13:1,5

and authorities at work. To question authority was akin to rebelling against God.

Since Mike was the Senior Pastor, his word became law. When he said "jump!" our response was, "how high?" He was *God's man*, so we obeyed.

As the teachings of the shepherding philosophy took hold, I worked night and day to please Mike. Ironically, the scripture teaches that submission to human authorities is something we do toward God, not as a means of gaining favor from human leaders. Before long, we became professional *brownnosers*.

I lived to make sure Mike's wishes were carried out to his complete satisfaction. In time, I became known as "*Little Mike*." We did not look alike, but church members understood that dealing with me was like dealing with Mike. I mirrored his attitude and opinions. Loyalty became my passion and priority.

As time went by, Mike promoted other deacons to eldership. A unique comradery developed among us which governed how we spent each day. We lived in a *covenant* relationship with each other. That meant we sacrificed, played, prayed, and laughed together. We also shared our resources as needs arose.

Some elements of this practice reflect the model of Acts 2:44: *"And all the believers met together in one place and shared everything they had."* In this passage, Christ-followers demonstrated astounding generosity toward each other. Because of this, many non-Christians saw the love of God in action.

In our case, a covenant relationship was more like a contract. We owed allegiance and loyalty to one another above family and above all other bonds. Ultimately, we were not connected by the love of Christ necessarily, but adherence to the covenant itself.

To Pay or Not To Pay

One of our leaders owned a farm with several acres. In prayer one day, he felt that God wanted him to donate it to Good News. Mike gladly accepted the offer and plans were made to re-purpose this property to become our ministry headquarters.

At the same time, Mike decided to try his hand at education, so we opened a small church-based elementary school. I relocated to an apartment near the main headquarters. My job was to help administrate the new school when not tasked with carpentry work on the new property.

My weekly salary was fifty dollars each week. Our ministry was a "faith" ministry, so if funds were available, I got paid. If not, I lived by *"faith."* If the check did not come in, I could not pay the rent. My *faith* meant the landlord would have to understand my circumstance and do without the rent money. Because the apartment owners also attended Good News, they put up with this arrangement.

Sometimes, my situation became so dire that I went without food altogether. Complaining was not an option. Other workers at Good News suffered the same shortages. I accepted this situation as part of the ministry.

Mike raised funds to refurbish the buildings on the donated land to build offices and a residential facility for teenage boys. We wanted to create a program similar to Teen Challenge, founded by David Wilkerson,[3] one of Mike's heroes.

We raised thousands of dollars and excitement increased while we worked side by side to refurbish the farmhouse towards the grand opening. Then a bombshell dropped.

To everyone's dismay, Mike changed plans and decided to move his own family into the newly renovated facility! He justified his decision by claiming that his growing family needed space. Extra funding would be required to build quarters for the teens.

---

[3] Worldchallenge.org

Many people expressed concern (these were the days before nationally televised scandals became common). As grumbling increased, Mike announced during a church service that, *God told him to move his family to the church's headquarters.* If others disagreed, it was just too bad!

The next week, he moved his family to the new facility. He forced "God's will" on the church refusing to permit anyone to take part in the decision, sending a clear message: To reject his edicts was paramount to rejecting God.

From that point forward, Mike's housing, food, and daily needs came out of the general fund. Besides that, he paid himself a salary twenty-five percent higher than all other workers.

Soon, Mike drove a brand new car. His family dressed in the latest fashions. Unfortunately, ministry employee incomes and situations remained the same. One pastor on staff received $300/week to take care of his large family. Adjusted for inflation, this would equal about $30,000/year in today's dollars.

In addition, the staff all missed about a third of their paychecks each year. On December 31st of each year, we signed a giant check for the amount lost back to Good News. We never had an option to refuse.

By signing these large checks, it appeared that we got appropriate compensation but knew otherwise. Our bills would go unpaid so the ministry could look reputable.

Since submission to authority remained a top priority, few dared to question these decisions. Mike was God's man. Our duty was to obey his directives.

Some of you read this and may question our sanity. If you've not been in a similar situation, it is difficult to fully explain. Good News did not deteriorate overnight, but gradually.

Most of us are familiar with the frog in the kettle analogy. You can boil a frog alive if you turn up the heat slowly. The frog keeps adjusting its body temperature never realizing it is being cooked to death.

If you were to expose a frog to boiling water quickly, it would feel the danger and escape. Like the frog, many of us didn't recognize that spiritual danger was increasing until it was too late.

Mike viewed challenges to his authority as spiritual rebellion. As mentioned, the shepherding movement emphasized "covenant relationships." Covenant relationships meant God linked us to each other. To abandon or violate the relationship covenant with one another was akin to breaking our covenant with God.

As a result, we felt powerless to oppose our pastor. When you combine his height and deep booming voice, Mike intimidated everyone but the bold.

Questioning Mike's authority on any issue cost you. Either he humiliated you in private or publicly spoke about your actions in a general way during a future sermon. He was not a man who forgave those he viewed as "rebellious."

On a few occasions, some members tried to suggest a viable system of accountability. Each alternative met obstinate resistance from Mike. "He built the church," so who were they to question?

As an elder and eventually an ordained pastor, I wondered what role I played to confront this bad behavior. I felt trapped by my own beliefs.

Good News had no appeal process. There were no independent advisors who could address problems within the leadership. We just bit down hard and moved on.

I do not believe Mike intended to deceive people. Like us, he thought that the teachings of the Shepherding Movement expressed God's will and purpose. Rather than measuring these teachings against scripture, we accepted them without question. Mike felt that his function was to train us to live by submission teachings.

The principles upholding a pastor's absolute authority evolved into a particular term. He called it, *"New Testament Order."*

Whenever Mike saw slippage in ministry income from the offerings, we preached *NTO* to bring people into compliance with our interpretation of scripture. Rebellion of any kind was a violation of NTO which we interpreted as violating scripture itself.

Mike's lack of training and connection to other churches meant doctrinal errors like this would go unaddressed and uncorrected. As a result, Good News pointed toward a downward spiral.

The Power Of Sympathy

The same day Mike moved his family into our new headquarters, he fell victim to a hereditary disease requiring constant attention and medical care. The caused regular pain and discomfort.

As a result, Mike was often irritable and exhausted, since he was required to go to the hospital several times each week. Even so, he soldiered on believing it was God's will for him to lead the church into the future.

Church members felt terrible about the suffering Mike had to endure on a daily basis. He was our spiritual leader. We empathized with Mike and his family throughout this nine-year ordeal.

On an individual basis, people made extra efforts to help ease the strain. People bought him gifts, gave love offerings, and did what they could to make his life easier.

The sympathy his disease engendered also created an untenable situation. Mike was seldom available to make executive decisions. As a result, many serious issues remained on hold for months.

No one dared to challenge him, fearing they would add more stress to his life. As a result, we became even more accustomed to "acting" like everything was great. It wasn't.

As a church, we acted like children of an alcoholic. Everyone tiptoes around an alcoholic, fearing he or she might get angry or out of control.

In substance abuse homes, other family members adopt a calm attitude fearful that the perpetrator might do something rash. We experienced something similar.

Anyone meeting with Mike seldom brought terrible news. They would find ways to represent problems in a positive light to keep him happy. As an unintended consequence, Mike was therefore shielded from reality by those around him.

No one wants to confront a sick man. Who wants to be the one who brings stress into an already stressful situation? When Mike taught or did something unethical, we tended to look the other way in the name of mercy towards his condition.

We who remained faithful to Good News respected and loved Mike. We had seen all the positive things he had accomplished. He dedicated his life to serving God. We were the beneficiaries of his vision and persistent quest to share the gospel.

Church members prayed for him and his family throughout this extended ordeal, holding all-night vigils and days of fasting. People far and wide prayed for miraculous healing from God.

At the same time, many of us resented the fact that the illness itself enabled Mike to wield absolute power. Because people felt sorry for him, they accommodated his every desire.

For example, one day Mike was bored and asked me to take him for a drive. We wound up at the horse track. Initially, Mike said that he just wanted to grab some lunch and watch the animals run.

Before his conversion, Mike loved to gamble. After lunch, Mike asked me to place two bets for him. I knew this was wrong, but his illness combined with his authority put pressure on me to do what he asked. It was the first (and thankfully last) time I placed a bet on an animal!

As "luck" would have it, he won the daily jackpot! He was ecstatic even though it only yielded a few thousand dollars. He gave me a $100 and tipped the person at the counter though he never met her.

Desperately in need of funds, I accepted the gift and became complicit in the whole affair. Then he asked me, *"Now did God or the devil cause me to win?"*

I did not reply. In a way, Mike bought my silence when I accepted the money. However, if I could respond today, the answer would be, the devil.

Mike gave back the money he won by frequent return visits to the horse track with his sons over time. This living on the edge of sin philosophy opened the door to test other ethical boundaries that impacted us all.

New Testament Order came to dominate every sermon, irrespective of who preached. This emphasis minimized other valid teachings from scripture.

For example, if preaching was about family, submission within the family was the main point. If the subject was spiritual warfare, the emphasis centered on lack of submission to elders...and so forth.

We also took lots of offerings. It was not uncommon to receive at least two offerings during each service: One for general expenses and another to fund:

- A new building program
- The pastor's love offering
- A new bus
- New outreaches.
- Children's ministry programs

Mike's family members managed all funds collected in the offerings. No one dared question whether this practice was ethical. No one wanted to be considered a rebel or trouble maker.

Financial decisions rested exclusively with Mike. The pastoral team and deacons had no say about how funds got dispersed.

The immediate effect of this practice kept the majority of spending directed towards the needs at headquarters. Outreach centers received little or no assistance for expenses beyond rent and utilities. Simple expenses for coffee, refreshments or church stationary came from the pockets of staff.

Consequences

Without minister friends for counsel, Mike relied upon his *street smarts* to lead the church. He adapted his experiences in the music and business worlds to create unique ministry applications to outreach. Sometimes these innovations were tremendously successful. At other times, not so much.

The ministry chose new leaders based on loyalty to the written and unwritten rules of Good News Chapel. Once selected, our mission was to serve whenever called, irrespective of our circumstances. There was no schooling, training or mentoring. We had to figure it out for ourselves.

I needed extensive training. My calling was clear, but my experience was nonexistent. The best track for me *might have been* to enroll in classes. However, Mike had no training either, so he lacked the foresight to create or develop a system to establish new leaders. In many ways, we were the blind leading the blind.

In spite of this weakness, we genuinely believed that Good News was superior to all other churches in the region! We thought we possessed a heavenly hotline to God, so we felt free to judge other pastors and churches in a negative light.

The seeds of our destruction grew and bore fruit as the years went by. Members believed that serving Mike's needs was identical to serving Christ. While the Bible teaches us to honor those in spiritual authority,[4] God never intended that church members become indentured servants.

With teaching about submission so prevalent, people felt insecure to make their own decisions. People went to Mike to get approval for basic questions like:

- What car should I buy?
- How much money should I put in savings?
- Should I date this girl/guy?
- Should I take this job or another?
- Should I buy a house or rent?

Church members increasingly depended on Mike for every choice in their lives. We devolved into a church filled with immature adults, incapable of making even the smallest decisions.

Consider the ramifications of men and women afraid to make adult choices without getting approval. We must've seemed like fools to the outside world.

---

[4] Hebrews 13:7

Hair Today, Gone Tomorrow

This need for approval revealed itself on men's faces. Mike wore a mustache, so guess what? Seventy-five percent of the men in Good News sported mustaches under their noses. Facial hair became a symbol of loyalty and allegiance.

Is anything wrong with wanting to imitate a church leader? No, but you must admit, this practice was just a little creepy! Culturally, this occurred at a time when mustaches were uncommon in society, so we tended to stand out.

The mustached considered themselves part of the inner circle. It reminded me of a Dr. Seuss book[5] when citizens defined status in life as wearing a star on their belly! This striving for approval did not stop with men's faces.

Scores of late model Volvos lined the church parking lot. Mike had two, I had two, and each elder had at least one. The local dealership loved Good News Chapel. Mike enjoyed Volvos, so we did too! No reflection on Volvos - they are a great car - but our goal was to adapt ourselves to his likes and dislikes in every possible way.

Those wanting Mike's approval went out of their way to take care of whatever needs he had. Men competed to wax his

---

[5] The Sneetches and Other Stories by Dr. Seuss, pub. 1953.

car each week. Others bought expensive gifts for Mike or Christine at Christmas time with funds they did not have.

Mike never demanded these things. However, the teaching coming from our pulpits made heroes of those who performed these acts of kindness.

Also as mentioned, the church gave Mike a monthly "pastor's love offering" on top of his regular salary. Keep in mind; the ministry paid all his expenses without impacting his paycheck.

One way leaders tried to curry favor with our pastor was to report on the words and activities of other members. Over time it became clear that a key way to gain favor with Mike was to provide information about members no one else knew.

Those loyal to Mike became unofficial spies. They kept track of church members who acted in ways that violated Good News policy and reported all infractions directly to Mike.

In abusive systems, inside knowledge is power. As elders, we provided observations and juicy tidbits about other church members. I say now with absolute shame that I would betray my fellow elders on any level if I saw them violate our unwritten and arbitrary rules.

Mike did not intentionally form this system, but it was a natural outgrowth of a doctrine that had gone to seed. We genuinely thought we did God's will by acting in this manner.

As a result, a deepening sense of paranoia developed. Everyone in authority watched everyone else! Friendship took a back seat to loyalty. Were we a church or the KGB?

[Before you continue, download chapter four from
ministerstoolbox.com/free-courses.]

THE RELATIONSHIP CONUNDRUM

Good News began and flourished through relationships. In the early days, Mike and Christine befriended a lot of young people. They hung out together, talked and laughed together, and went everywhere together. This approach embodied the Jesus People revival of that era.

Gradually, Good News became more formalized. We grew from a simple coffeehouse to a multi-church organization spread across our state. Size required we create procedures, rules, and systems so that the ministry could make a more significant impact.

Proper organization and administration is not a hindrance to the Holy Spirit. Administration is a gift from God.[6]

---

[6] I Corinthians 12: 28.

Organization and administration become obstacles, however, if they supersede the importance of relationships.

Fueled by a misapplication of submission and authority, dating relationships became rare in Good News. When you consider how many young adults attended the church, this situation was bizarre.

To date a member of the opposite sex, you needed Mike's approval. Allow that to sink in for a moment.

Scripture teaches Christians not to bind themselves into dependent relationships with unbelievers.[7] Paul, the apostle, applied this principle to business partnerships and dating relationships. If we place ourselves in binding relationships with those who do not follow Christ, we hinder our mission in life.

Non-Christians are not motivated to respond to the direction of the Holy Spirit. In a marriage or business alliance, therefore, a Christian will always be forced to divide their priorities.

In our workplaces, most of us do not choose those we work alongside. This verse speaks of circumstances when the choice is under our control. Paul warns us not to *yoke* or legally bind ourselves to people who declare different loyalties.

---

[7] II Corinthians 6:14

Beyond this principle, Mike felt it was his duty to sign off on each dating relationship in the church. Over time, this went further than the faith of both parties. The relationship needed to look and feel right to him. Many relationships did not pass the test.

On occasion, Mike suggested who would make an appropriate match. When coupled with everyone's extreme desire to please the pastor, you can imagine the unintended consequences. Even if two people were not attracted to each other, they felt the pressure of a "God-ordained" relationship.

The Road To Marriage

When deciding to date my wife, I had already learned the system through a great deal of personal pain. When I first saw my wife, I couldn't take my eyes off her but knew I needed to play it very cool. I did not even address her verbally for more than two years!

When I gathered the courage to ask her out finally, I first chose a time when Mike was in a good mood and prayed *a lot!* I was keenly aware that Christine had someone else in mind for me. However, I was able to navigate Mike's O.K stealthily by waiting for him to be in a good mood.

After securing his tentative approval to begin dating, I needed one more consent. Thankfully she gave it!

As juvenile as this sounds, Patricia and I dated and told *no one*. We avoided each other's company at church. I seldom spoke to her in front of other church members and even kept my eyes looking elsewhere during services.

Why? I had witnessed many relationships go south by a slip of the tongue or a perceived inappropriate behavior. The dating culture at Good News was oppressive, but I was determined not to become another victim.

After six months and a dozen dates, I once again sought out that particular time when Mike was in a good mood. I prayed a great deal and when the time was right told him that I wanted to pop the question. Without consulting his wife, Mike essentially gave me license to do what I thought best.

At the next church meeting, Mike announced our engagement to the shock of nearly everyone. Most people congratulated us, but we also received our share of icy stares. It appeared that we both broke some hearts that night, though we could not fathom how things would soon unfold.

Pat and I then started to plan our wedding day, but there would be landmines along the way.

The Blues

My fiance loved the color blue. In scouting out a place for our reception, she found a hall nearby which had everything she desired. The cost of our reception out the door was $8.00/plate. The going rate at the time was $15-$20.00 (Yes, I'm that old!)

We were both thrilled as plans appeared to be falling into place. Pat's family began to make preparations, design invitations, and other wedding-related details.

A week or so later, Mike asked me about our plans for the reception. When I told him about how we found "the blue room," he became angry.

He concluded that such a place was far too lavish for a pastor in Good News. Either I canceled these plans, or the wedding was off! (Keep in mind that Pat's father planned to fund the entire reception. It would not *cost* us anything.)

Mike wasn't the only one upset that day. When I conveyed his edict to my fiancé, she burst into tears. *What had we done wrong?* Her non-Christian parents didn't know what to think. It was all so absurd.

From my vantage point, we had three options:

1. *Lie and tell Mike that the reception was set and refuse to back down.* This would facilitate my immediate removal from ministry and the loss of all our Christian friends overnight.
2. *Elope.* Same as above, but bring additional hurt to our families.
3. *Submit myself to my pastor without resistance like a good dog.* (Something I was expert at doing.)

I selected option number three. When the smoke cleared, we would have the reception at the place of Mike's preference: a large town hall that was significantly less elegant!

Following Mike's advice, we contacted *his* chosen caterer. I was not permitted to hire a band, so we did not have to worry about the dancing portion of the festivities. Instead, we could use a portable boom box for music. Our three hundred guests would be served soda, water, or coffee since wine was also not permitted.

The new location was inconvenient to all our guests, except Mike's family. Following his directions, I chose Christine's brother for my best man. Fortunately, he was a friend, but not my first choice.

Plenty of other landmines were detected and neutralized along the way. From years of experience, I knew the system.

To achieve our goal, we would have to keep smiling and moving forward no matter what obstacles came.

On the day before our rehearsal, Mike was taken to the hospital, ill. While this was not necessarily unusual due to his frequent illnesses, both my fiancé and I had a distinct feeling that he did not want to do the ceremony anyway. Patti had not been his "choice" for my life mate.

A fellow pastor would stand in for Mike and perform the ceremony. Thankfully, God paid attention to all these setbacks. In spite of it all, He gave us great grace.

We Now Pronounce

Unbeknownst to us, God moved behind the scenes. A week before the wedding, the town brought in contractors who applied fresh paint to the walls and sanded the old wood floors. By the day of our wedding, the formerly dingy hall looked and smelled brand new.

The wedding ceremony went well and almost without incident. No one seemed upset at the reception venue, as relatives enjoyed each other's company. The lack of dancing or alcohol went mostly unnoticed. Many later reported that ours was the best wedding they had ever attended! Now that's grace!

After the reception, my brother drove us thirty miles in the opposite direction to see Mike. We walked into his hospital room, just as he was expressing disappointment that we had not bothered to visit him on our wedding day!

Moments later, we walked into his room in full wedding regalia. He let out a yell heard throughout the ward, and the nurse came running. Tears flowed as he congratulated us again and again.

I include this addendum to the ceremony for you to witness the complexity of my pastor. One minute, he was a dreaded foe. The next moment, a generous friend.

After the honeymoon, we came home and moved into our apartment. Pat worked for an insurance company which accounted for most of our income. The outreach center I led was forty-five miles from headquarters, so most of our early days together were spent driving to and from the church.

In those early newlywed days, Mike pulled me aside and strongly advised me to wait one year before starting a family (And no, I'm not kidding). As both of us were in our late twenties, this counsel fell on deaf ears.

As time went on, these intrusions into my private life became ridiculous. After the ordeal we went through with our wedding, Mike's personal opinions started to have less and less of an effect on our thinking. We decided that his wishes for our family were outside the prevue of his pastoral authority.

Sure enough, Pat became pregnant with our first child after six months. Mike was noticeably angry, viewing this pregnancy as a rebellion against his authority. For more than a month we endured the cold shoulder treatment.

No congratulations. No inquiry into common courtesies customarily given to those with such great news. What should have been a joyous occasion was greeted with dismay.

Finally, one morning, when all the other leaders were present, Mike posed a question to me.

"So, Mr. Sabella. How do you intend to pay for this new arrival?"

His question went right to the heart of the matter. Since my meager salary came from the church, Mike felt like HE had another mouth to feed!

My response surprised him and changed the atmosphere permanently. I replied, *"The same way I've paid for everything else in my life: By faith."*

My response seemed to please him. From that day on, he welcomed the idea of my assuming a daddy role and soon gave me a raise!

Additional Breaking Point

I will never forget Jimmy, an older man who served as a deacon in our church. For years, Jimmy had been a pillar in the church, ready to help anyone, any time. Many of the young people at Good News saw him as their spiritual grandpa and included him in all their activities.

Mike had an old friend who sold cars and began attending Good News Chapel. When Mike learned that Jimmy was looking to purchase a used automobile, he sent him to his friend's dealership.

After taking a look at the cars on the lot, Jimmy decided he was not interested and went home. He also did not relate well to Mike's friend, the owner, feeling pushed to buy something he did not want.

This information all got back to Mike, who then called me to the office with Jimmy. There, he excoriated him for insensitivity to the situation. Mike told him to apologize immediately to his friend! Though he stated again and again that he did not want to buy a car from his old friend, Jimmy was removed from the diaconate for refusing to comply.

I stood there in horror and silence as Mike attacked this godly man. I knew my pastors violated half a dozen scriptures, but my fear of recrimination overshadowed my will to do something about it.

Jimmy left the church soon afterward and in a few years fell victim to Alzheimer's disease. When I last visited him, he recognized no one and died a few years later.

Jimmy was my wake-up call. I could not justify what I saw biblically and knew I owned some of the blame for refusing to speak up. To restore my conscience, I could no longer look the other way. I need to take personal responsibility.

Other occasions arose when I was sent to rebuke an errant member or take actions that were unethical. In the early days, I just did what I was told believing that God would honor me for obeying His chosen leader. Now, I could not stomach my cowardice.

The incident with Jimmy changed my perceptions forever. What was I doing? How did shaming a servant of God match scripture? My conscience hurt a long time after Jimmy got sick. I knew I needed to start taking a stand for righteousness.

Marriage had a positive effect on me because I now had a friend to confide in and share these concerns. Though my new wife was alarmed to hear about some of these occurrences, she remained supportive, prayerful, and focused toward helping me do the right thing.

Conflicts increased between Mike and me that are too obscure to relate. The result of these constant battles was my eventual removal from board positions and responsibilities to the mother church. Ironically, this gave me the freedom to focus more on furnishing our apartment and preparing for our first born since I had more time away from headquarters.

Since I no longer 1 held a position on any board, the relationship between Mike and I began to improve. I cannot explain why. Perhaps he saw that in spite of our differences, I was not running out on him. As mentioned, I genuinely loved the man, warts and all.

Over the next few months, the bond between Mike and I got reestablished on a different level. From my vantage point, it felt like the early days of Good News Chapel.

When our daughter was born, Mike gave me a raise and gleefully announced our new arrival to the congregation. Soon afterward, the time came for us to dedicate her publically.

With family and friends surrounding us, Mike prayed a blessing over her young life. Little did we realize at the time that this would be his final church service.

[Before you continue, download chapter five from
ministerstoolbox.com/free-courses.]

GETTING THE FULL PICTURE

G ood News Chapel began with amazing promise driven by a vision to reach thousands with the gospel.

However, here is a brief overview of the ministry just a dozen years later:

1. **Church Meetings**. Each member traveled up to one hundred and twenty miles round trip to attend several church meetings each week. No excuses were acceptable except illness. Those who missed a meeting faced potential confrontation. Sermons criticizing the uncommitted became frequent.

2. **Maintenance**. Deacons and elders devoted Saturdays to doing repairs and upkeep at the church-owned property where Mike lived. The requirement was non-negotiable to serve in ministry. Every week we mowed lawns, painted, and

made general improvements to the property which became a working farm.

Volunteers vacuumed and washed floors. The less favored shoveled manure off the fields into one designated pile. The reason we did this? *"To be a better witness to the community."* Anyone who desired to serve in future leadership roles adjusted his/her schedule accordingly.

Keep in mind that these *requirements* began as acts of love and service to Christ. When we acquired the farm, skilled members volunteered to help. They built fences and made improvements. Over time, this volunteerism degenerated into mandatory "work days."

There is nothing wrong with church members pitching in to help the physical needs of any ministry. Thank God for people who care enough about their church to volunteer. Churches could not accomplish very much without the dedication of faithful servants of God. In our case, volunteerism gradually became servitude.

Many church members left their lawns uncut or yards unraked to fulfill their responsibilities to Good News. Our church property looked fantastic while members' homes were in dire need of maintenance.

3. **Compensation**. Full-time staff was alarmingly underpaid year-in and year-out. College educated, state-

certified school teachers got paid minimum wage or less. Each employee of Good News missed several of their meager paychecks each year due to lack of funds or other priorities.

During those years, church-owned livestock ate the best hay and grain. Mike's family drove the most beautiful cars, wore the latest fashions, and enjoyed the benefits of upper-middle-class wealth.

How could such inequities continue? Remember the frog analogy? These practices did not happen overnight, but gradually.

Sacrifice is a real part of Christian ministry. There are times when funds are low, and churches struggle to make ends meet. Unfortunately, Good News failed to provide appropriately for their key people year after year.

Staff scraped and hustled to meet their own pressing needs for housing, clothing, and food. Still, Good News was able to display an image of wealth and abundance to the community.

4. **Dress Code**. Leaders were required to wear tee shirts and sweatshirts bearing our children's ministry emblem. Its cartoon design was perfect for kids but made adults look foolish; sort of like clowns.

On Bible Study nights, the church filled with adults wearing bright yellow attire. A smiling penguin on the front advertised Good News Chapel. We were like walking neon signs.

Leaders who did not wear this clothing could expect an angry confrontation from Mike. On one occasion, I was bawled out for wearing a blazer that covered part of the emblem on the shirt. I was commanded to remove the blazer and return to the meeting to join the other neon signs.

5. **Funding**. Staff pastors delivered all offerings from our network of outreach centers to headquarters each week. Local assemblies had no authority to determine how money was spent in their respective regions.

Headquarters paid the bills for the rent, mortgage, and utilities of each center. Any additional expenses had to come from the pockets of regional pastors. Only select family members had access to the financial records of the ministry.

For example, as pastor of one of the congregations, I did not have the power to buy letterhead for my church. Headquarters trivialized requests like these as unnecessary due to more pressing obligations. What were some of these more pressing obligations?

- New saddles and headgear for the horses stabled at headquarters.
- Painting of existing buildings every two years whether they needed it or not.

- Purchase of an elaborate pony cart for recreational rides around the property.
- New fencing for the livestock.
- Construction of storage buildings – which remained 90% empty.

Mike directed all purchases. After expenses, all additional funds were used to improve headquarters. Since all outreach centers remained financially dependent on the "mother" church, real growth was difficult if not impossible.

One incident illustrates how "submission to authority" became so out sync with Christ's teachings.

When Good News decorated its new facility at headquarters, Mike wanted a cross to adorn the wall. He decided that the gold cross hanging on the wall of one of our other outreach churches would look better in the new building.

The cross had been part of the original church's history for eighty years. Someone invested a lot of money at one time to make the cross the central focus of the front of the sanctuary.

One Sunday, the gold cross disappeared and suddenly appeared on the front wall of the new sanctuary at headquarters. For many weeks, the outreach pastor was embarrassed to explain the ethics of taking this action, which could not be justified.

As a replacement, a wooden cross was crafted by one of the members to replace the gold original. No matter how everyone felt, we all agreed that the gold cross *looked much better* in the new facility than in its former home. In essence, as leaders, we all gave our consent to *theft!* These events seem absurd, yet they occurred.

Another Point Of View

As the reader, you may be asking a few things, like, why did people put up with all this? To answer that question, it is essential to paint additional brush strokes on the canvas that was Mike. He was an amazingly complex leader, himself compromised by the doctrines he had embraced as true. For example, he:

- Couldn't drive by a teenager selling her body to feed a drug habit without bursting into tears.
- Was a creative genius, able to craft practical ways for non-believers to connect with the church.
- Had a disarming sense of humor and could be uproariously funny.
- Raised money for other ministries just because he liked what they were doing in other parts of the world.
- Loved his family and believed he was doing what the Bible taught.

- Could be your greatest friend or your most determined enemy. You would love him and hate him; sometimes in the same day!
- Possessed an understanding of spiritual things at times that would amaze you. Moments later, he would act so childish you wondered if he ever had met Christ!

God worked through this man in extraordinary ways. To this day, some people look back at Mike with unabashed fondness and affection. To them, he was their pastor, beginning, middle, and end.

I understand. Difficult as it may seem, I count myself among them, but now with eyes wide open.

[Before you continue, download chapter six from ministerstoolbox.com/free-courses.]

THE PHONE CALL

I will never forget that day.

Pat and I were finishing up new parent chores when the phone rang. On the other end, a fellow pastor was calling, but his voice was abrupt. Something was wrong.

He called to inform me that my pastor had just passed away.

Honestly, I was stunned with disbelief. Mike had gone to the hospital countless times for one reason or another through the years. All night prayer vigils for his recovery became commonplace, followed by many miraculous healings.

As a group of churches, we became accustomed to hearing about how God intervened. This time, his heart gave out fighting the disease that weakened his body each day. Still, his death came as a total shock even though he was sick so often. As leaders, we became accustomed to receiving instructions. Now our leader was gone.

Hundreds attended the wake and funeral over the next few days. People came from far and wide to pay their respects. We all stood around trying to be helpful but in shock. As pastors, we did not consider or plan for this eventuality.

Mike never discussed with us how the ministry would continue without him. In retrospect, this was probably by design.

At the time of his death, the church operated through two separate tax-exempt corporations. Good News Chapel was the "spiritual" arm of the organization.

Our three-man pastoral team was responsible for preaching and taking care of counseling congregational members with personal problems. We provided spiritual direction for all the churches.

The men's program operated through a separate corporation that also had responsibility for all property, administrative and financial decisions.

Mike's family members governed this second corporation. In the days leading up to his death, we never questioned why the ministry was designed this way. We just followed instructions.

Without Mike's presence, we believed our immediate task as pastors was to form a human shield around Mike's family. Our goal was to make sure that the ministry continued to support Mike's vision spiritually and financially.

This approach worked for a few months. Staff got paid regularly, which was a positive change. Each pastor focused more time and attention serving their outreach centers instead of headquarters. Long hours spent in staff meetings or helping Mike overcome his daily physical challenges were no longer necessary.

Cracks in the Foundation

As pastors, we began to discuss many of the excesses and ways Good News was failing in its mission to make disciples. We realized that as a ministry, we needed to get back to the church's mission to reach new people, or we would not survive.

The family had a different view. They felt their mission was to keep things exactly as Mike left them. To do otherwise would dishonor his memory from their perspective. A collision was inevitable.

Over time, the goals of these two ministries came into conflict. As leaders, we couldn't do outreach without money, but the other corporation controlled the purse strings. Concerns would be taken under advisement, but the primary objective seemed aimed at keeping everything the same.

Though Mike had not given the pastors guidance about how the ministry would function after his death, he did set the stage for what unfolded next.

During the final years of his life, he gave his family members "secret" information. These *secrets* were the weaknesses or sins he either knew about or created around perceived threats. Ironically, he disclosed this strategy to me once when he voiced concern about another leader.

In the event of future conflicts, Mike wanted his family empowered to stop any opposition that might arise from the pastors! These *secrets* were designed to intimidate and ultimately ruin the credibility of anyone who did not remain loyal to the family.

I became the first to voice disagreement with some of the directions and practices of the ministry. The family was not pleased.

Before an evening service I was threatened that if I did not back down from voicing my concerns, salacious personal information would be disclosed to the church.

This threat did not frighten me since I knew the information was groundless. I knew Mike created several stories out of thin air if necessary to ensure his family would be protected. When confronted, I decided that yielding to such threats was not going to happen.

Minutes later, immediately following evening worship, I stood up in the congregation and publicly resigned. People were stunned. They had no idea of the trouble brewing behind the scenes.

I knew at that moment that the ministry could not survive. You cannot treat people this way and expect God's hand of blessing to continue. I walked away from Good News that night a free man (or so I thought) for the first time in many years.

Neither Patti nor I shed tears. Instead, we felt a deep sense of relief. The cycle of compromising and living a lie ended. We could be ourselves, and our faith felt stronger than ever.

Since my outreach center was so far from headquarters, they merely unplugged it from the larger church. I was now responsible for rent, expenses, and income. That suited me fine.

The other two pastors stayed in touch with me, but soon the rumor mill went into full swing. A few weeks later, another pastor resigned following a similar conflict.

The third pastor stayed for several months attempting to keep the ministry together to honor Mike's memory. Eventually, he left as well. When he did, many of the remaining members went to his home and pledged their support if he decided to start a new church.

He did.

Outwardly, the family expressed no concern after we resigned. They did not fathom the central role pastors played in the longevity of the ministry.

After hiring a new pastor, they believed the church would fill up again with new supporters and that life would go on. They were in for a big surprise.

Good News sputtered under the weight of a severely reduced budget. Without free labor, the ministry and its men's programs closed its doors forever two years later.

The rumors that surfaced from our resignations destroyed many long-standing friendships. Even now, decades later, there remain former members who will not speak to me due to the misinformation they received.

For a long time, the property stayed vacant. Over the years, weather and wild animals ruined many of the buildings. Finally, a horse farm bought it for pennies on the dollar.

Years later, an enterprising contractor purchased the property once again, demolishing the old structure and restoring the remaining buildings. Today, there is no evidence a church ever existed on the property.

[Before you continue, download chapter seven from ministerstoolbox.com/free-courses.]

I LEFT THE CHURCH, BUT THE CHURCH DIDN'T LEAVE ME

nvested 15 years of my life into Good News Chapel. My best years went toward building a ministry that was doomed to collapse under its own weight.

My wife and I spent many years serving an organization that lost its mission and purpose. We wasted time doing farm chores instead of reaching people for Christ. Our passion centered around enforcing man-made rules and regulations instead of proclaiming the Word of God.

We wanted to get busy reconnecting with a more biblical model of Christianity.

During this hiatus of personal reconstruction, I often thought about how refreshing it was to be free. No more pretending everything was all right. No more struggling with my conscience or preaching messages to get more money in the offering.

In many ways, I felt as if I had been born again – again! I cannot express the pure pleasure of pastoring a small church and focusing on local issues. During Mike's life and the aftermath, much of my time was spent traveling to headquarters to attend meetings of one sort or another. Having the freedom to use the funds from our local offerings to plan for the future was a great joy.

Anxious to get my church on track and mission, I introduced changes in my church to become more relevant to our locality. We dismantled ineffective programs and invested more time and money into marketing our church and the ministries we offered.

The former pastors of Good News continued to meet weekly. We were each living in a brand new reality. We were not accustomed to making leadership decisions on our own, strange as that may seem. Our training was to follow orders, not design solutions. We soon discovered that trying to stay united as pastors presented unique challenges.

Since each congregation was located in a different city, churches had distinct demographics, issues, challenges, and passions. Previously, we met together based mainly on our history, but that was disappearing into the rearview mirror. As a result, our assessments of how to lead our congregations began to clash.

My primary gift is teaching. Within that gift is the ability to perceive the future if current practices remain the same. (Sort of like envisioning what a building will look like if you keep adding floors).

I could *see* that this arrangement had no future in its present format.

Making corporate decisions about what we all would do together when each church was so fundamentally different made no sense to me. We met regularly to discuss issues common to our churches, but had less and less in common! Therefore, I resigned *again*.

I hoped to continue forward and relate to the other pastors collegiately, but not be bound to a covenant that I viewed outdated and unnecessary. Initially, they resisted, and many conflicts followed.

My intent was not to pursue isolation – quite the opposite. However, I wanted the right to make my own local decisions without checking with the other pastors for permission.

We never functioned independently before. In retrospect, we each needed space and time to sort out what happened to us. Thankfully; we all remain friends to this day.

Reality Isn't All It Is Cracked Up To Be

What I failed to realize upon leaving is how deeply affected I was from years at Good News Chapel. From my vantage point at the time, the cause of all our difficulties vanished when we departed.

All I needed to do was preach the gospel, and our small fellowship would explode with growth. To my surprise, this did not occur.

Like all churches, we had our own set of problems. Some of them frustrated me to no end. However, I could no longer blame Mike or Good News Chapel for our lack of progress. Frankly, that was annoying! We did not experience the growth I anticipated, and I did not know why.

Several months passed. One morning, I attended a pastor's seminar in a nearby city. There, the Holy Spirit unexpectedly met me. It was not through any specific teaching. Instead, by a combination of things I cannot fully explain, God revealed what held us back.

The Holy Spirit revealed that *I left Good News Chapel, but Good News Chapel had not left me.* It was a thought that hit me like a ton of bricks. As I sat considering it, revelation flooded my consciousness.

Thoughts raced to the forefront of my mind confirming that I had not changed much since leaving Good News. Like the Israelites, I came out of Egypt, but Egypt did not come out of me.

I arrived at Good News as a teenager and left in my early thirties as a family man. The examples of how to live the Christian life developed by Mike's preaching and example.

How I thought, reacted, responded, and decided was deeply affected by daily exposure to the philosophies driving my former church. The good, the bad, and the ugly all combined to form what I became as a minister. Though I'd left the premises physically, much more work was ahead of me to preserve the good and reject the bad.

Without realizing it, I still judged people unfairly, just like my former pastor. I got angry when things didn't go my way – just like my former pastor. Many of my methods remained similar to those practiced at Good News.

I still viewed people as sheep who could not make life decisions without my guidance. If they did not seek my advice, I saw them as unspiritual.

I still expected subservience from those *under* me. It was upsetting when people did not address me with the title, "Pastor."

If people called me by my first name, I became annoyed, believing they were disrespecting me. Though scripture warns about this attitude,[8] somehow I thought it did not apply to me. I *deserved* respect, and that meant people would need to call me pastor or reverend.

I also became angry when members did not fully dedicate their time and efforts to the vision of our church. People were either *with* me or *against* me. Performance mattered most, not a person's circumstances.

I considered congregants as a means to an end, not a flock entrusted to me by God. Unfortunately, I continued to surrounded myself with those who thought and acted just like me.

Without realizing it, I was building my own little Good News Chapel, not the kingdom of God. My unrecognized enemy stared me in the mirror each morning, and I did not like him very much!

It dawned on me that I could no longer blame Mike or Good News for my behavior or attitudes. The comfort of blaming people or circumstances no longer applied. God

---

[8] Matthew 23:8-10

wanted more from my life. Was I willing to face the mirror and make changes?

Friendships Fail To Materialize

Jesus told his followers: "...You are my friends..."[9] Jesus made developed new relationships all the time. He was accessible. Even children spontaneously ran to him in the middle of his sermons.[10]

He enjoyed meals with people, listened to their stories, and basked in the company of those considered *common* by the elite. Jesus was so approachable that disciples felt confident to give him advice![11] In most cases the opinion was wrong! Still, they felt close enough to Christ to offer their ideas regularly.

At Good News, Mike established his ministry on the foundation of faulty teaching. We all did. His opinions about friendship and how pastors interact with their congregations did not serve him well. Instead, these beliefs and ideas chained him to a lifestyle that ultimately lead to fear and loneliness.

---

[9] John 15:14
[10] Mark 10:14
[11] Matthew 16:22; Luke 9:12

Those under his leadership experienced the same results. Mike often said,

"As a leader, you cannot be friends with your people."

He believed, practiced, and suffered from this philosophy. Mike's ideas about friendship caused paranoia to flourish throughout the ministry. In reality, he was deathly afraid of losing control.

Scripture does not teach leaders to be separate from their congregations. Christ modeled the opposite. Jesus and his disciples walked, ate, laughed together, and sat around fires every night. He never endorsed isolation from his followers.

When I left Good News, I discovered that pastors of many denominations unconsciously held the same ideas as my former pastor. They were afraid to become too close to their congregations or fellow ministers fearing vulnerability.

Pastoring is a unique function in the body of Christ. We are called to lead people toward Christ and wholeness. Along the way, people can be very unkind, so it is easy to retreat emotionally and keep people at arm's length.

Unfortunately, this coping mechanism is unhealthy and leads to isolation and loneliness. We all know that the way predators attack and kill sheep is by teaming up to separate them from the flock. Satan uses this same strategy to destroy leaders by urging them to disconnect from other believers.

Apart from a lack of training, Mike struggled with many personal and family issues. Without people he could trust, he made foolish decisions that wasted resources.

Good News had people with excellent skills. School teachers, technicians, accountants, and tradespeople offered their services free of charge. We squandered these gifts by assigning them to do farm chores. Amazing skills could have advanced the church and helped our leadership grow.

Proverbs declares: *"...in an abundance of counselors there is safety."*[12] None of us sees the entire picture.

Counselors are friends. They are people we trust for advice. Other Bible versions translate the word *safety* as *victory*. Without friends, ministers have little chance of success.

I looked at my church and realized that I too, was going it alone. Similar to Mike, I also wasted the people and resources God entrusted to me.

Through prayer and study of scripture, I realized my life was out of sync. Leaving Good News Chapel was not the solution I thought it would be. I needed help!

---

[12] Proverbs 11:14b ESV

[Before you continue, download chapter eight from ministerstoolbox.com/free-courses.]

COURSE CORRECTION

*Like a fluttering sparrow or a darting swallow, an
undeserved curse does not come to rest.*[13]

Curses don't just appear. There is a reason why they come.

Deception came to rest in my life through a cause-and-effect relationship. When God drew up plans for me before my birth, He didn't decide I would become part of a cultic church.

Scripture tells us that everything God creates is good. He did not create me to twist, pervert or destroy my life with bad choices or teaching.

How God takes our lives and re-forms them as if it was His divine plan all along is beyond comprehension. Paul said,

---

[13] Proverbs 26:2

...and we know that God causes everything to work together for the good of those who love God and are called according to his purpose...[14]

Curses came into my life through deception. I fell into deception for reasons I will now explain. God did not lead me into error - Casey did. The Bible teaches that every person must face this reality to experience lasting freedom.

The Dad Thing

My father grew up during the Great Depression of the 1930s. Times were tough outside the home, but even worse inside. My dad and his father had a poor relationship. His house was a battlefield, where arguing and fighting became the norm.

During the Depression, my grandfather disappeared for two years without a trace. My grandmother, dad, and aunt were left to fend for themselves. When grandpa reappeared, he never explained his absence but pretended like everything never changed.

The damage to the family and the pain each member endured stayed private. Family members just moved on.

---

[14] Romans 8:28 NLT

My father grew up with a strong sense of insecurity. He vowed to himself that he would never be poor again. He would never abandon his family like his father.

Dad reached his goals in life. He became a successful businessman. Along with his childhood sweetheart, he raised a family of five boys and one girl. The difficult relationship dad experienced with his own father dramatically affected his ability to fill the role of dad himself.

True to his convictions, he did not repeat his father's mistakes. Ironically, many of his sons grew up with varying degrees of bitterness towards *him.*

Dad conquered the poverty which caused his shame and embarrassment. The unresolved relationship he had with his father passed through to most of his children.

Growing up, I was the angriest of the lot. Though I seldom engaged in drinking or drug abuse, dad questioned whether I would survive until my eighteenth birthday. We had a rocky relationship as far back as I can remember.

If he said "black," I said "white." When he went left, I went right. I cannot recall a time as a child when I *liked* my dad. He provided food, clothing, schooling and many other privileges most kids dream about, but I could not wait to be free of him.

When Jesus found me at seventeen, I was not the warmest guy in town. As you've learned, Christ changed all that.

Well...most of it.

People share their experiences of receiving Christ into their hearts. Each story is unique. Some feel burdens lift or dramatic changes in circumstances. My story is that the bitterness that dominated my world just vanished. I could feel it go.

When my father learned of my conversion, he was both thrilled and mystified. Excited, that the course of his son's life no longer headed towards self-destruction. Mystified, that I would choose to follow Christ of my own free will!

Arriving home after visiting my brother, he saw a total change in my countenance. The hate was gone. Love from God extended out through my words and actions. He truly was stunned.

Holding Pattern

Airplanes remain in holding patterns if airport sky traffic is congested. When runways become available, traffic controllers signal the plane to stop its holding pattern and come in for a safe landing.

When I arrived home, my brother and I scouted for a good church. We both settled on Good News Chapel, even though it was several miles from home. I *loved* the church. Most in attendance were my age and came from similar backgrounds.

Christ cleansed me from bitterness against my parents. Still, the habit patterns of resisting authority remained intact.

Though the hate was gone, I stayed in a holding pattern of sorts. I no longer hated my parents but did not know them or love them either. After leaving Good News, God decided it was time to restore a healthy relationship with my father.

My former church was not equipped to train rebels since Mike was a bit of a rebel himself. Though I no longer hated my dad, I did feel comfortable judging him as a "pagan!"

When my parents did not accept my message about Jesus for themselves, I devalued them in my mind.

I grew up in a culture and era that celebrated rebellion. The media represented rebels as independent and powerful. I'm not sure much has changed! Young people ridiculed authority. Honoring parents, police officers, or the elderly as God commands was considered anachronistic.

Our pastor struggled through his issues with authority. This reality created the perfect environment for deception to grow.

It is possible that Satan stayed coiled in the background during those early years of ministry. Perhaps he waited until we gained a reputation in the region. Then he could yank the rug out from underneath us, using our folly as his most potent weapon.

At conversion, God intended to renovate my belief system. Problems with authority did not disappear when Christ came into my life. Instead, they remained in a holding pattern until I was ready to listen.

A New Approach

The Holy Spirit started to "nudge" me. Do you know what a nudge is? Its kind of like everything you read and hear about all at once seems to have the same emphasis. In my case, the message was to initiate time with my father. Even though I was married with two children, God seemed intent on repairing our relationship.

At the time, my parents owned a second home in Vermont, so I asked him if he would like to go skiing. Since this was a question that came out of the blue, he seemed uncomfortable with the concept. What was I planning? Was this another attempt to convert him to Protestant Christianity?

While I assured him there was no agenda, he invited my sister along as a buffer. We skied and enjoyed the weekend. I think he kept waiting for the "conversion talk." It never came.

On a second trip during the Christmas season, we had some long discussions. I held nothing back about my negative experiences at Good News Chapel and elected to give him access to the real me, without any hidden motives. To my surprise, he reciprocated.

At the end of the trip, over a dinner of fresh fish, he delivered the knock-out blow. He said, *"You know, I never liked you as a kid growing up. But, after today I want to tell you that I love you."*

What do you say to that? *"Pass the ketchup, please?"* Little did I know; this was the beginning of God's process to not only restore a broken father-son relationship but also break rebellion's grip over my future.

Soon after this event and knowing his love for golf, I decided to learn the game myself. Judging from the look on my father's face when I asked him, I believe he saw a vision of angels!

None of his children played or ever expressed interest. Within moments he provided an extra set of clubs and set me up with lessons from his golf pro.

Over the next few months, we grew closer together through the catalyst of golf. I never posed a threat to Tiger Woods, but I gradually learned the fundamentals of the game.

One day, dad and I played nine holes at a course designed for more experienced golfers. Our habit was to play without a cart, allowing us to walk and talk.

After the first few holes, I started to impress myself. That was about to change.

On the sixth hole, I scored a twelve! The seventh, a ten and it would not get better as we went. By the end of the game, I couldn't wait to toss my bag in the car and head out for a bite to eat.

Dad was not so inclined. *"Bring your pitching wedge, and let's go to the practice green,"* he said.

He might as well have said, *"Let's go to the Tower of London. I want to offer you a haircut."* I had no desire to comply but followed him anyway.

My father's teaching methods were direct and not altogether pleasant. From his vantage point, I would stay at the practice green until my golfing skills improved. If I did not follow his instructions, I could enjoy criticism until I did. To most people, that would not seem like a big deal. To me, it was pure pain.

On the practice green, he watched every move I made. When I did not follow instructions, he let me know in his colorful way.

His goal was noble enough. He did not want to see his son lose unnecessary strokes during future golf games.

From my perspective, that practice green exposed my rebellion against God's authority. You see, I never followed my father's advice growing up. His methods tended to be cutting, sprinkled with choice curse words. This time on the practice green made me feel like a three-year-old receiving punishment all over again.

So, here I was a thirty-four-year-old pastor and father of two learning the fourth commandment.[15] I knew my heavenly father orchestrated all of this. Emotionally, I felt like bucking his advice and ending the day in an argument. I knew that God had something else in mind.

I made a conscious decision that day to submit myself to his instructions in spite of his teaching methods. It was time for me to grow up and listen to direction regardless of how it was delivered.

God gave me my dad. It was God's design to place me under his authority. By rejecting that authority, a void developed that led me toward many poor choices. The fourth

---

[15] Exodus 20:12

commandment promises us that honoring our parents causes life to "go well" for us. The opposite is also true.

Rebellion against authority cannot be cured. We break its control by deciding to submit ourselves as if we were submitting ourselves to Christ Himself.

During that half an hour of instruction, I kept my mouth shut and listened to his advice. I gave it my best effort to learn what he offered.

I left the golf course that day a changed man. All those wasted years of broken relationship with my earthly father started to heal and fill needs I did not know I had.

Passing On The Genes

During the time my father and I were building this new relationship, his father passed away. I cannot say that I was close to my grandpa as a child. We saw him on holidays. He was a gregarious man; loud and fun-loving in his own way, but I did not connect with him on any level.

The funeral was indeed a surreal experience. At a certain point, my dad invited me to join him at the open casket. As he looked upon the lifeless body of his father, he said these fateful words:

"God have mercy on your miserable soul." Well, *that* was a special moment!

As mentioned previously, my dad's home life growing up was turbulent. On at least two occasions, the end of an argument between father and son concluded when my grandpa said, *"I disown you!"*

Unwittingly, my grandfather exercised his parental authority to pronounce a curse over my dad's life. Since neither served the Lord, they did not recognize the conversation as anything more than an argument. Nevertheless, a life-changing curse occurred in the spirit realm.

My dad's hatred for his father boiled into a rage. Getting away from home became my father's passion. When WWII broke out, he lied about his age and joined the Navy at sixteen years old.

Upon returning home, dad went to college and hustled his way through two universities to earn two degrees. There are many stories within all that worth discussing, but too long to tell.

He married his childhood sweetheart, moved to another state, had a boatload of kids and became successful in business. Though my grandfather eventually expressed pride in his son, the relationship never addressed the pain between them. They tolerated each other, but never became close.

At the funeral, my father returned a curse upon his father. Unknowingly, that curse had already passed to the next generation. I grew up despising *him* even though he never disowned me.

When I heard this pronouncement over his father's lifeless body, something clicked inside of me. I knew then that the curse must stop or the same fate awaited my own family. It did not matter that I was Christian now. Reversing the curse was essential.

Our relationship as father and son continued to develop and grow through the remainder of his life. I kept lines of communication with him and enjoyed stopping by the house during the week for a bowl of his home-made soup and chat about things that mattered to both of us.

Many times, he told me point blank that he loved me. Unsolicited, we embraced often. In his later years, he made it a point to say to me that he was proud of me.

What changed? I did not teach him this. As God repaired our relationship, Satan found no stronghold to gain influence.

Without noticing, the restoration of our relationship changed something in my psyche forever. The need for affirmation or recognition by other leaders diminished. National movements lost their fascination for me.

I was no longer drawn to strong, authoritative figures because truth be told, I was no longer seeking or needing a father figure. The desire for recognition that often comes from a broken relationship with a father disappeared.

In its place, God gave me a healthy respect for other leaders, but also an understanding that they were neither superior nor inferior to me. I respected them because of Christ's hand on them, not from a need to be accepted.

At first, this freedom was difficult to explain to people who knew me. I came to understand that trying to conform myself to any movement or person is unnecessary for walking with Christ.

God has graced me with a deep love and appreciation for leaders. Because of the insights Christ gave me, I am not afraid to speak to anyone, anywhere about anything when prompted by the Holy Spirit.

In my current ministry, I do not aim to gain acceptance per se but to strengthen other leaders who serve His Kingdom. Because of what I have been through, I became comfortable in my own skin.

Many years later it fell to me eulogize my father at his funeral. It was a fantastic experience to sum up our relationship. Through tears, I spoke blessing over him again and again. Forgiveness and the power of Christ broke the curse over my children. By honoring my father as the fourth commandment instructs, we changed a distant relationship to love.

[Before you continue, download chapter nine from ministerstoolbox.com/free-courses.]

CAN YOUR CHURCH BE REPAIRED?

You picked up this book because you have concerns about some of the practices in your church. Perhaps you have experienced things that cause you to wonder. Does your church have solvable problems, or is it broken beyond repair?

I shared my story to allow you into my life on a very personal level. I do not speak clinically, but from a place of experience as a congregant and also as a leader. That said, it is *always* your responsibility to judge correctly whether anyone's ideas or counsel matches the heart and will of God for your life.

The Church is Christ's greatest love. He died to create it and makes himself available to her 24/7. All human history culminates in the Church's ultimate completion at a heavenly ceremony between Jesus and his Bride.[16]

His Church is a collection of people from many backgrounds and cultures. Denominations, titles, buildings, and programs have little significance in Heaven.

Millions of people <u>form</u> this unique organism. They are weak, strong, broken, heroic, male, female, young, old, sick, and healthy, but loved by the Father through receiving His Son.

All churches have problems. The letters by Paul, James, John, Peter, and Jude all address problems in regional churches. The issues run the gamut from sexual impropriety to false doctrine to abuse of spiritual gifts and laziness in the workplace.

As long as we are humans, problems will abound. Much of the entire Bible is designed to address issues before they arise. Issues don't destroy churches - unless they remain unaddressed.

Leaders are appointed by God to create solutions that reflect God's purposes for the local church. However, leaders are flesh and blood, so the solutions are not always perfect.

---

[16] Revelation 21:9

Signs Of A Healthy Church

The following are structural principles. In themselves, they do not guarantee a church will be healthy but form the foundation for ensuring a church stays on track.

Health is an organic term. It signifies that relationships among church members closely match New Testament examples of community among believers (Acts 2:42-46). Jesus spoke of his disciples as friends.[17] This is the model of any true New Testament church.

Health also represents that church members understand and enjoy a personal relationship with Christ. Teaching centers around the person and work of Jesus. His substitutionary death on the cross and resurrection are at the heart of why believers gather.

A house of worship can be administratively brilliant, yet still be spiritually dead. How? The church is alive. It is not a machine, but a *body*. It is living, so while we all desire efficiency, we cannot allow the form to replace organic life.

That said, four structural principles help ensure a church will have the tools necessary to resolve conflicts and keep it

---

[17] John 15:14

on track for long-term growth. These will give you a framework to determine the health of your church.

1. Finance

How are offerings collected? How are they spent? Who is responsible for bookkeeping? What measures of accountability are in place?

One financial expert told me that he could understand everything about a company without ever meeting a single employee. All he needed was to examine their ledger. From their expenditures, he could describe their moral convictions, philosophy of leadership, and dozens of other attributes. His point: what we do with money as individuals or churches defines us.

Churches that become abusive always mismanage money. Resolution is possible if this is due to carelessness or ignorance. At other times the motivation is intentional and should raise a red flag.

Here are some fundamental safeguards to prevent mismanagement in any church:

- Collect offerings and assign at least two people to verify the amount and sign off on each deposit slip.

- Dismiss immediate family members of church officials from financial responsibility to alleviate suspicion.
- Submit the bank statements and financial records for a yearly audit to an independent accountant or CPA.
- Develop written policies concerning how money is collected and dispersed. Include these policies in the Constitution and By-Laws.
- Acknowledge individual contributions yearly by January 31st of the following year as a minimum standard and to comply with federal law.

God entrusts church leaders with the funds given by His people toward the work of the church. Congregations should be squeaky-clean regarding they spend the funds. Members should have access to a yearly report.

Smaller churches will spend the lion share of their income on facilities and staff. This practice is normal. As the church grows, goals should be set to increase the percentages for outreach and mission.

Members should not have access to exact salary amounts. Why? Pastors like all employees have the right to personal privacy.

Because his/her salary comes from the church, a small representation of a board or governing body should work with pastors and staff to make sure they are paid generously to meet their daily needs.

2. Clear Mission

Healthy churches know why they exist. What has God asked your church to accomplish in this generation? Is there clear evidence the church is moving toward that goal?

In his book, *Good to Great*,[18] Jim Collins speaks about the priority of placing people in the right positions. The analogy he uses is a bus.

Effective leaders get the wrong people off the bus, the right people on the bus and then assign them to the right seats.

Once accomplished, they can formulate a clear mission. If leaders function in the wrong seats, the church mission will remain ambiguous.

Congregations become unhealthy when they turn inward and ignore people outside the church. Several denominations exist today who once were passionate about the unchurched, but now only care about maintaining their current buildings and serving their members.

---

[18] Copyright 2001 by Jim Collins. All rights reserved.

Is your mission clear to everyone? Is it clearly stated in your literature, social media, website, from the pulpit, and in all your contact with the outside world?

Churches can be reinvigorated by just getting back to their original mission and eliminating whatever detracts from it.

In growing churches, the mission is uncomplicated and easily repeated by anyone who attends. Effective missions closely align with the Great Commission[19] to have lasting value.

3. Leadership Structure

Churches have come under greater scrutiny today due to the myriad of scandals that have rocked the religious community over the past several decades. Some allegations have been unfair and untrue, but others warn us to be careful who we assign to this critical role.

Healthy churches establish standards and practices to ensure accountability and invite creative solutions to problems in the decision-making process. If a governing church board is comprised of several family members, the likelihood of fairness and integrity reduces dramatically.

Depending on the denomination, leadership teams can be formed from titled (pastors, deacons, sextants, elders) or

---

[19] Matthew 28:18-20

untitled (directors, board members, etc.) officials. Governance should set clear guidelines regarding behavior and character in keeping with Paul's instructions.[20]

Leadership also creates the culture of a local church. Culture by definition is a set of shared attitudes, values, goals, and practices that characterize a church. Why is culture important?

Clear guidelines and values help eliminate confusion or miscommunication. Questions church leaders should discuss and agree upon include:

- Does the church require membership? If so, what are the benefits and responsibilities?
- Do congregants vote on crucial decisions? If not, what process enables a non-leader to share ideas or suggestions?
- What are the steps to become more involved or serve in some way? Are there different standards for serving in the music ministry or finance ministry?
- What is acceptable regarding dress code? If a young man or woman becomes a regular attendee but wears revealing or inappropriate clothes, does the church have a process for dealing with each person fairly?

---

[20] I Timothy 3:1-13

- What is the procedure toward people who interrupt services with questions or arguments?
- Does the church have an understood policy when someone informs a member of your team that they are thinking of hurting themselves, committing a crime, or thinking of suicide?
- Can anyone in your church use your facility for personal use? If members want to use the church building for a wedding, is there a cost and what requirements must be met?

These are just a random sampling of issues that come up from time to time. Healthy church leaders discuss and decide on best practices before they occur.

4. Clear Appeal Process

Jesus foresaw regular conflicts taking place among his followers. In Matthew 18:15-17, he taught his disciples how to resolve disputes and disagreements among themselves.

> *If one of my followers sins against you, go and point out what was wrong. But do it in private, just between the two of you. If that person listens, you have won back a follower. But if that one refuses to listen, take along one or two others. The Scriptures teach that every complaint must be proven true by two or more witnesses. If the follower refuses to listen to them, report the matter to the church. Anyone who*

refuses to listen to the church must be treated like an unbeliever or a tax collector.

People have actual conflicts. This is part of real life. Every church has differences of opinion because humans get involved! Healthy churches take steps to resolve disputes. Unhealthy churches ignore conflicts enabling a state of denial to develop.

Paul warned the Hebrew Christians:

Watch out that no poisonous root of bitterness grows up to trouble you, corrupting many.[21]

The proper way to address conflict is to keep it private. One of the significant weaknesses I see in many churches is that we obey Jesus's words, but only *after* we violate them!

For example, we disagree with someone. Instead of following Jesus's method, we gossip to our friends, relatives, and everyone else unrelated to the problem. By the time we speak with the original person, rumors have developed, sides have been chosen, and the discord is a hundred times larger.

Jesus commanded us to get alone with a person when there is a conflict. Get things worked out one-on-one, approaching them with humility and a willingness to listen. Ask them if

---

[21] Hebrews 12:15b

they are aware of the infraction and discuss how it impacted you. This is how Jesus wants us to resolve problems.

If the discussion does not settle the dispute, invite others to get involved forming larger circles. If one of the participants refuses to forgive or do what is right, a separation may become necessary.

This biblical method applies to all believers, including those who serve in leadership. Healthy churches create an appeal process; somewhere to go when a congregant cannot resolve with the leadership team. In denominational churches, this usually involves a representative from headquarters.

In non-denominational churches, an appeal board can be comprised of respected leaders or pastors in the region who serve as advisors. Inviting trusted leaders builds trust and community. In their role, they can bring independent clarity to severe problems.

Wise leaders create this board or group early in the developmental stage of a church to safeguard truth and design protection for both leaders and church members. Healthy churches provide avenues of appeal. They genuinely desire to be accountable to God.

As we have discovered, all churches have problems. And while this may be hard for you to accept, you are either part of the problem or part of the solution. You're part of the problem if sinful behaviors continue, and your silence communicates tacit approval, thus enabling sin.

You become part of the solution when you decide to meet with leadership and design an appeal to resolve the problem(s).

I continue to serve as a church leader to this day. If someone comes to me or desires to meet with our leadership team to discuss some difficulties with the way things run, I can tell you approaches that will be problematic:

- Pointing out what is wrong without first asking questions.
- Showing a lack of respect for authority.
- Becoming argumentative at the first sign of disagreement.
- Threatening to leave the church if things do not change.

People who act this way do not follow the spirit and nature of Christ. Appeals are motivated by a love for Christ's church. To design one takes careful consideration and labor. Here are some key steps:

- Collecting data: Are rumors circulating around the church or region true? Do you have proof from at least two witnesses?[22] *"Someone heard that..."* is not a valid biblical source.

- Do you know all the facts concerning a recent decision or merely assume you do? Be open to the possibility that you don't have all the information.
- Do you know why events happened in the church as they did? Is the leadership able to provide an answer without jeopardizing privacy?
- In the event of a violation, do you have a redemptive solution to the problem? Are you willing to volunteer time or resources to help?

When trying to fix problems in your church, you must eject personal prejudice. If you are angered or moved by rumors alone, then your appeal will be in vain. Due diligence means you investigate what is right and separate it from what is false.

As a pastor, I have had several occasions when a disgruntled member has used misinformation, slander, and innuendo to attempt to derail a church I have pastored. They did not honestly investigate before they arrived at conclusions.

Paul frequently warned against individuals whose attitudes and beliefs undermine the faith of others or cause division.[23]

---

[22] I Timothy 5:19
[23] II Timothy 4:14, Titus 3:10, 3 John 1:9

120

Keep in mind that Satan's chief aim is to destroy churches, so do not approach this process lightly. The objective is God's glory, not hurting people or their reputations.

Once you collect all the data, meet with the leadership in a spirit of humility. God graces the humble but resists the proud. Humble means you open your heart and mind to the possibility that you may be wholly or partially wrong.

During an appeal, ask critical questions and be prepared to help if needed. It is not appropriate to say, *"This church does not reach new people."* Instead, what solutions do you offer to change this condition? Are you willing to invest yourself in helping turn things around, or do you only want to criticize? Jesus said,

> And why worry about a speck in your friend's eye when you have a log in your own? How can you think of saying to your friend, 'Let me help you get rid of that speck in your eye,' when you can't see past the log in your eye? Hypocrite! First get rid of the log in your own eye; then you will see well enough to deal with the speck in your friend's eye.[24]

I cannot speak for you, but if I have something in my eye, I won't ask a stranger working on a car engine to see if he can remove the dirt from it! Like yours, my eyes are very susceptible. There are few I would trust to help remove an obstruction.

[24] Matthew 7:3-5

Jesus teaches us that to be heard; we must be willing to listen. Do we see a speck in the church's eye when a beam is in our own? Are we critical of the pastor's family when our own family is not doing their part in supporting the church financially?

It doesn't take intelligence to point out problems. Anyone can do that. Are you prepared to be a part of the solution?

Churches with problems are normal from a New Testament perspective. If leadership is willing to listen and discuss ways to improve, that is clear sign that the church is salvageable. The greatest obstacle to church health is an unwillingness to consider obvious problems or attempt new approaches.

You should understand that not every idea, suggestion, or initiative will or should be implemented. Part of the leadership role is to discern both what is appropriate and what is timely for the congregation. Healthy churches are led by leaders who are willing to listen and consider alternatives genuinely.

If you continually receive stubborn resistance and unwillingness to provide basic answers to essential questions, you may be dealing with a problem church. These kinds of organizations are broken at a systemic level and cannot be repaired unless there is a change in leadership.

If you do not serve in leadership, then it may be time to consider other options.

[Before you continue, download chapter ten from ministerstoolbox.com/free-courses.]

LEAVING A CHURCH PROPERLY

The Church is a volunteer organization. As mentioned previously, it is Christ's chief love, even with all its defects.

On a local level, the church is also a family. That is why disconnecting from a church can feel like a divorce.

You worshipped and shared meals with other members. You shared life, striving to fulfill the same mission. To suddenly stop attending and go elsewhere will have relational ramifications.

You've read my story. Perhaps you see problems in your church that alarm you. You believe it is time to act for either your mental health or the good of your loved ones. If you have given these matters careful thought and prayer but can find no other recourse, it might be time to leave.

Leaving a church can be heart-wrenching. The possibilities for misunderstanding abound. Of supreme importance is that you do what you believe honors Christ best. In the future, you want no regrets or nagging sensations that you conducted yourself inappropriately. Leave a legacy, not a reputation. As Paul taught us:

> *Make every effort to keep the unity of the Spirit through the bond of peace.*[25]

This charge by Paul is difficult to carry out. When arguments or gossip are commonplace in your church, it is easy to fall into the same ungodly patterns when leaving.

One leader I knew who needed to leave his church due to a myriad of systemic problems said to me, *"I jumped into a mud hole to rescue people but got filthy myself."* In essence, by fighting, striving and arguing he did not change his church but sullied his reputation.

You may be in that place where despite your best efforts, there doesn't seem to be any other options to investigate. If after careful prayer and consideration you conclude you must leave, do your best to create an atmosphere in which

---

[25] Ephesians 4:3 NIV

reconciliation might take place in the future. That is what *"making every effort..."* demands.

How you leave depends mainly on the commitment you have with the church's mission. For simplicity's sake, I categorize these levels of responsibility into three stages.

Stage One

The *getting-to-know-you phase* of church involvement. You visit a church, begin to know a few members of the congregation and listen to the preaching. Perhaps you volunteer to serve at an event or two but have not committed yourself to the church yet.

While attending, you begin to notice certain teachings that do not match your understanding of scripture. Perhaps you ask questions of other members or staff to get clarification. Maybe not.

People become church members based on relationships, not doctrine. Because the internet is accessible 24/7, the best preaching and teaching is always available. Folks return to churches because they like the people who attend. They view that church as a place to develop friendships.

If you are in this stage of church connection and discover control, abuse, or doctrinal error, the solution is simple. You vote with your feet! Whether or not you wish to confront leadership with your concerns is entirely up to you, but this stage requires no obligation on your part.

Stage Two

At this juncture, you have given your life to Christ and become a water-baptized member. Your relationship with the church is more profound. You describe the congregation as "your" church rather than the church you attend.

Leaving your church at this stage is more gut-wrenching. You have invested time, effort, and money to help fulfill the mission. You have developed relationships with other members and identified those in authority as your leaders. Leaving the church in this stage is more complicated.

If you have seen and heard things that trouble you, Jesus' instructions from Matthew 18:15-17 that we discussed earlier, apply.

As you remember, this passage addresses broken relationships in the church. In stage two, you go to someone to get a problem acknowledged and resolved.

Your church or pastor may not have wronged you personally, but this principle still applies. As a member, make an appointment with the leadership to discuss your concerns. Ask for clarification on either the teaching or behaviors you find troubling.

As you speak with leadership, be prepared to offer alternatives. It is easy to point out flaws in a church since every church has them. Be helpful. Perhaps your input can bring change.

If you attempt to address the leaders, but experience ridicule for your concerns, action is needed. It may be time to resign your membership and find another church. Neither you nor your family should remain in an environment that is spiritually unhealthy.

Stage Three

In this scenario, you are like I was. You serve in some leadership capacity with responsibilities to your congregation. The principles of Matthew 18:15-17 still apply, but you should take more deliberate steps.

As a leader, you no longer answer for your involvement alone. By accepting a leadership role, you represent the interests of the local church. The reputation of that church is inextricably intertwined with your reputation.

To leave because of a disagreement or difference of opinion is not ethical because you are responsible to other members as a leader. Addressing the issues which are wrong, falls on your shoulders as part of your calling.

Churches do not go from preaching the gospel to preaching heresy overnight. The changes happen more gradually. I played a crucial role in empowering heretical practices and teaching by my silence and unwillingness to take a stand. By so doing, I failed God and His Church.

In the final years of Mike's life, disagreements between us increased to the point that he removed me from any supervisory role. When I look back, I wonder what might have occurred had I fought harder to demand more ethical standards. Perhaps Good News might have changed; maybe not. Unfortunately, I will never know.

Catherine the Great is quoted as saying, *"If you can't be a good example, you'll have to be a terrible warning."* I cannot speak for you, but I don't want my life or church to be a warning. I want my life's work to be a blessing. Paul told Timothy,

> In a large house there are articles not only of gold and silver but also of wood and clay; some are for special purposes and

some for common use. Those who cleanse themselves from the latter will be instruments for special purposes, made holy, useful to the Master and prepared to do any good work.[26]

God desires that we become vessels of honor in his house and according to this verse, we get to choose. As a leader, we can be negligent and hide our heads in the sand. That adds up to wood and clay. Or, we can follow our consciences and stand for what is right no matter what the cost. That becomes gold and silver.

Leaders lead, and if that is His calling upon your life, you must get used to standing alone when circumstances demand. The great thing is that if you stand up for Christ, He promises to stand alongside and speak through you by His Holy Spirit.

As someone who has served in leadership all of his adult life, I hate to see anyone disconnect from a church. However, when you do with is right before God, sometimes that is the only godly choice.

[Before you continue, download chapter eleven from ministerstoolbox.com/free-courses.]

---

[26] II Timothy 2:20-21 NIV

LESSONS LEARNED

I have now had thirty years to look back and reflect on my experiences at Good News Chapel. Even now, the final chapter is yet to be written.

Many who were children at the time of these events grew up nearly oblivious to what I have just described. They look back on Good News Chapel with fond remembrance. Their memories describe a jovial man with a great vision who loved Christ.

I cannot argue with that assessment. Mike loved kids and did all in his power to reach them for Christ. Though I have laid out some difficult history here, my purpose is not to stain my former pastor's legacy, but to provide help to those going through similar problems in their church.

Mike became deceived by accepting false doctrine as truth. He was sincere and sacrificed a great deal to serve in ministry. In spite of his mistakes, we will reunite in heaven. Of that, I have no doubt.

In spite of the history shared in these pages, I loved the man. God used him to impart several principles into my life that remain to this day. For example:

- Mike let no obstacle stand in his way to achieve what he believed to be God's will. That same drive has characterized my ministry over the years as well.
- He was fearless and did not respect one man over another. To this day, I am never nervous around any leader, no matter who they are.
- Mike stepped out in faith to do great things. I am not as bold, but daunting challenges do not deter me.
- As ironic as it sounds, Mike preached that the Word of God trumps everything and everyone. I received that truth early on, and that principle guides my steps until this day.
- Mike did not change his personality when he stood behind a pulpit. That lack of "performing" remains important to me, and I have difficulty listening to those who do otherwise.

These are just some of the ways God used him to shape and influence me. Though Good News veered off track, I learned through the years to,

"Chew the meat and spit out the bones."

One of the significant struggles you will encounter in leaving an unhealthy church is sorting through the rubble to preserve what was right. Our natural inclination is to reject everything from that experience, but we need to take time in prayer and scripture study to hold on to what is right.[27]

Turn Mistakes Into Opportunities

Blame is just another word for unforgiveness. Many have experienced greater abuse than what I've discussed in this book. Unfortunately, when they finally get free from the church organization, bitterness and confusion govern their lives for years. These emotions ruin the present with memories of the past.

When people don't address what attracted them to abusive leadership in the first place, they will either abandon the faith or find another abusive leader. Time and experience have revealed this truth again and again.

No matter what was done to you, take responsibility for the part *you* played. You may have been cautious to speak up like I was, but silence in the face of abuse is a sin. Owning up

---

[27] I Thessalonians 5:21

to what we did or failed to do enables God to do his work in our hearts and character.

I do not mean that you trust those who wronged you. Forgiveness can be offered, but trust must be earned. God endorses proper boundaries in relationships throughout scripture.

If you have experienced an emotional assault by a church leader, pray for the perpetrator and release them to God. If you played a role in any part of the incident, ask God to forgive you. You do this for both God and yourself.

In the Lord's prayer, He taught us that we would be forgiven in the same way we forgive other people. Unless you release them by choosing to forgive, they will continue to control your present and your future.

I can share with you that my passion for serving God is just as real as it was when I first joined Good News Chapel as a teenager. To be sure, these events have sharpened my discerning skills, but through forgiveness, I have discovered that my faith remains unharmed.

The experiences at Good News gave me a sixth-sense for people in danger of false teaching or spiritual abuse. Because I have seen first-hand what wrong teaching can do, my ears perk up if I hear a sermon or teaching that is just a little off.

Many times, I have conversations with people who spent time in problem organizations or even cults. They all think I was a fellow member! Several former Jehovah's Witnesses were surprised to learn that I've never stepped foot into a Kingdom Hall.

My experience taught me that cultish behavior is more widespread than we may think. Leaders inside and outside of the church sometimes use manipulative techniques to achieve what they cannot acquire through integrity.

My experiences taught me to question doctrine and measure it against scripture more carefully. The goal now is to influence others to think more deeply about the consequences of what they embrace as biblical teaching. I can say as Paul did:

> *He comforts us in all our troubles so that we can comfort others. When they are troubled, we will be able to give them the same comfort God has given us.*[28]

In essence, because I have seen God use these events redemptively, I can help people going through the same struggles. Sometimes God graces me to bring correction to a leader or church to help them get back on track. Other times, I can assist those experiencing abuse to sort things out.

---

[28] II Corinthians 1:4

God indeed takes whatever challenges you have faced in the past, including negative choices, and transform them into opportunities to declare His glory. Paul said it this way in his letter to the Roman Christians:

> And we know that God causes everything to work together for the good of those who love God and are called according to his purpose for them.[29]

God can take any pain, any wrongdoing – on your part or others – and turn it around to honor Him.

These experiences (positive and negative) have made me a better leader (and hopefully a better man). I hope this small offering has begun a process of helping you sort out God's will and purpose for your life.

By no means can any book address every possible scenario. That is why I conclude with other books that may assist you in your quest to get the answers you need.

Thank you for taking the time to read this book. It has been a great honor to perhaps offer some help by addressing these painful issues. I encourage you to pray about the answers you gave during the course and ask God what steps or changes you might make in your daily life to serve him more effectively.

---

[29] 8:28

If you did not take advantage of this bonus, I urge you to reconsider and go back to work through the questions posed. These were created to help you make wise decisions about your present and future walk with Christ.

God bless you in your quest to serve the Lord.

-Casey Sabella

If you have suffered sexual or physical abuse at the hands of a spiritual leader, that is another realm entirely. You need to report such abuse to the proper civil authorities.

 Casey Sabella is a popular podcaster, author and speaker who has served in pastoral ministry over several decades. Together with his wife Patti, they have raised four children, who along with their spouses, all serve The Lord in ministry.

Though Casey continues to serve on the leadership team of a local church.

Other Books By The Author

Titanic Warning takes the reader through the historic journey of that ill-fated ship, examining the leadership styles of four captains. Each played a significant role in the doom or rescue of the survivors. *It is recently updated on Kindle.*

Discovering Your Ministry reveals how to begin serving God where you are in practical ways.

Additional Books Addressing Spiritual Abuse

- *The Subtle Power of Spiritual Abuse*, David Johnson & Jeff VonVonderen
- *Healing and Spiritual Abuse*, Ken Blue
- *Toxic Faith*, by Stephen Arterburn & Jack Felton

Future Books

Minister's Toolbox, a compilation of the best podcasts from his popular broadcast in written form. (May 2019)

Building A Strong Foundation helps new believers understand the basics of following Christ. (April 2019)

Prophetic or Pathetic, an examination of the gift and ministry of prophecy in today's church. (July 2019)

Contact Information

Casey currently serves as the Sr. Pastor of Motion Church (mymotionchurch.com). He is available to speak at conferences or church seminars from time to time. Contact him at casey@ministerstoolbox.com or @caseysabella.com.

Follow him on *Twitter* (@leadersministry) and Facebook (facebook.com/ministerstoolbox).

He hosts a regular podcast called Minister's Toolbox that helps leaders succeed in ministry. Available on iTunes and Google Play, or directly from ministerstoolbox.com.

Made in the USA
Middletown, DE
15 March 2022